Hunger

Hunger

A Memoir of (My) Body

Roxane Gay

W F HOWES LTD

This large print edition published in 2018 by
W F Howes Ltd
Unit 5, St George's House, Rearsby Business Park,
Gaddesby Lane, Rearsby, Leicester LE7 4YH

1 3 5 7 9 10 8 6 4 2

First published in the United Kingdom in 2017
by Corsair

A CIP catalogue record for this book is available
from the British Library

ISBN 978 1 52880 136 2

Typeset by Palimpsest Book Production Limited,
Falkirk, Stirlingshire

Printed and bound by
T J International in the UK
Printforce Nederland in the Netherlands

for you, my sunshine, showing me
what I no longer need and finding
the way to my warm

PART I

CHAPTER 1

Every body has a story and a history. Here I offer mine with a memoir of my body and my hunger.

CHAPTER 2

The story of my body is not a story of triumph. This is not a weight-loss memoir. There will be no picture of a thin version of me, my slender body emblazoned across this book's cover, with me standing in one leg of my former, fatter self's jeans. This is not a book that will offer motivation. I don't have any powerful insight into what it takes to overcome an unruly body and unruly appetites. Mine is not a success story. Mine is, simply, a true story.

I wish, so very much, that I could write a book about triumphant weight loss and how I learned how to live more effectively with my demons. I wish I could write a book about being at peace and loving myself wholly, at any size. Instead, I have written this book, which has been the most difficult writing experience of my life, one far more challenging than I could have ever imagined. When I set out to write *Hunger*, I was certain the words would come easily, the way they usually do. And what could be easier to write about than the body I have lived in for more than forty years? But I soon realized I was not only writing a memoir of my body; I was forcing myself to look at what my body has endured, the weight I gained, and how hard it has been to both live with and lose that weight. I've been forced to look at my guiltiest secrets. I've cut myself wide open. I am exposed. That is not comfortable. That is not easy.

I wish I had the kind of strength and willpower to tell you a triumphant story. I am in search of that kind of strength and willpower. I am determined to be more than my body – what my body has endured, what my body has become. Determination, though, has not gotten me very far.

Writing this book is a confession. These are the ugliest, weakest, barest parts of me. This is my truth. This is a memoir of (my) body because, more often than not, stories of bodies like mine are ignored or dismissed or derided. People see bodies like mine and make their assumptions. They think they know the why of my body. They do not. This is not a story of triumph, but this is a story that demands to be told and deserves to be heard.

This is a book about my body, about my hunger, and ultimately, this is a book about disappearing and being lost and wanting so very much, wanting to be seen and understood. This is a book about learning, however slowly, to allow myself to be seen and understood.

CHAPTER 3

To tell you the story of my body, do I tell you how much I weighed at my heaviest? Do I tell you that number, the shameful truth of it always strangling me? Do I tell you I know I should not consider the truth of my body shameful? Or do I just tell you the truth while holding my breath and awaiting your judgment?

At my heaviest, I weighed 577 pounds at six feet, three inches tall. That is a staggering number, one I can hardly believe, but at one point, that was the truth of my body. I learned of the number at a Cleveland Clinic in Weston, Florida. I don't know how I let things get so out of control, but I do.

My father went with me to Cleveland Clinic. I was in my late twenties. It was July. Outside, it was hot and muggy and lushly green. In the clinic, the air was frigid and antiseptic. Everything was slick, expensive wood, marble. I thought, *This is how I am spending my summer vacation.*

There were seven other people in the meeting room – an orientation session for gastric bypass surgery – two fat guys, a slightly overweight woman and her thin husband, two people in lab coats, and another large woman. As I surveyed my surroundings, I did that thing fat people tend to do around other fat people – I measured myself in relation to their size. I was bigger than five, smaller than two. At least, that is what I told myself. For $270, I spent a good portion of my day listening to the benefits of having my anatomy drastically altered to lose weight. It was, the doctors said, 'the only effective therapy for obesity.' They were doctors. They were supposed to know what was best for me. I wanted to believe them.

A psychiatrist talked to those of us assembled about how to prepare for the surgery, how to deal with food once our stomachs became the size of a thumb, how to accept that the 'normal people' (his words, not mine) in our lives might try to sabotage our weight loss because they were invested in the idea of us as fat people. We learned how our bodies would be nutrient-deprived for the rest of our lives, how we would never be able to eat or drink within half an hour of doing one or the other. Our hair would thin, maybe fall out. Our bodies could be prone to dumping syndrome, a condition whose name doesn't require a great deal of imagination to decipher. And of course, there were the surgical risks. We could die on the operating table or succumb to infection in the days following the procedure.

It was a good news/bad news scenario. Bad news: our lives and bodies would never be the same (if we even survived the surgery). Good news: we would be thin. We would lose 75 percent of our excess weight within the first year. We would become next to normal.

What those doctors offered was so tempting, so seductive: this notion that we could fall asleep for a few hours, and within a year of waking up, most of our problems would be solved, at least according to the medical establishment. That is, of course, if we continued to delude ourselves that our bodies were our biggest problem.

After the presentation there was a question-and-answer session. I had neither questions nor answers, but the woman to my right, the woman who clearly did not need to be there because she was no more than forty or so pounds overweight, dominated the session, asking intimate, personal questions that broke my heart. As she interrogated the doctors, her husband sat next to her, smirking. It became clear why she was there. It was all about him and how he saw her body. *There is nothing sadder*, I thought, choosing to ignore why I was sitting in that same room, choosing to ignore that there were a great many people in my own life who saw my body before they ever saw or considered me.

Later in the day, the doctors showed videos of the surgery – cameras and surgical tools in slick inner cavities cutting, pushing, closing, removing essential parts of the human body. The insides were steamy red and pink and yellow. It was grotesque and chilling. My father, on my left, was ashen, clearly shaken by the brutal display. 'What do you think?' he asked quietly. 'This is a total freak show,' I said. He nodded. This was the first thing we had agreed on in years. Then the video ended and the doctor smiled and chirped that the procedure was brief, done laparoscopically. He assured us he had done over three thousand operations, lost only one patient – an 850-pound man, he said, his voice dropping to an apologetic whisper, as if the shame of that man's body could not be spoken with the full force of his voice. Then, the doctor told us the price of happiness – $25,000, minus a $270 discount for the orientation fee once a deposit for the procedure was made.

Before this torment was over, there was a one-on-one consultation with the doctor in a private examination room. Before the doctor entered, his assistant, an intern, took down my vital information. I was weighed, measured, quietly judged. The intern listened to my heartbeat, felt my throat glands, made some additional notes. The doctor finally breezed in after half an hour. He looked me up and down. He glanced at my new chart, quickly flipping through the pages. 'Yes, yes,' he said. 'You're a perfect candidate for the surgery. We'll get you booked right away.' Then he was gone. The intern wrote me prescriptions for the preliminary tests I would need, and I left with a letter verifying that I'd completed the orientation session. It was clear that they did this every day.

I was not unique. I was not special. I was a body, one requiring repair, and there are many of us in this world, living in such utterly human bodies.

My father, who had been waiting in the well-appointed atrium, put a hand on my shoulder. 'You're not at this point yet,' he said. 'A little more self-control. Exercising twice a day. That's all you need.' I agreed, nodding vigorously, but later, alone in my bedroom, I pored over the pamphlets I had received, unable to look away from the before/after pictures. I wanted, I still want, that after so badly.

And I remembered the result of being weighed and measured and judged, the unfathomable number: 577 pounds. I thought I had known shame in my life, but that night, I truly knew shame. I did not know if I would ever find my way past that shame and toward a place where I could face my body, accept my body, change my body.

CHAPTER 4

T his book, *Hunger,* is a book about living in the world when you are not a few or even forty pounds overweight. This is a book about living in the world when you are three or four hundred pounds overweight, when you are not obese or morbidly obese but super morbidly obese according to your body mass index, or BMI.

'BMI' is a term that sounds so technical and inhumane that I am always eager to disregard the measure. Nonetheless, it is a term, and a measure, that allows the medical establishment to try and bring a sense of discipline to undisciplined bodies.

One's BMI is one's weight, in kilograms, divided by the square of one's height in meters. Math is hard. There are various markers that then define the amount of unruliness a human body might carry. If your BMI is between 18.5 and 24.9, you are 'normal.' If your BMI is 25 or higher, you are over-weight. If your BMI is 30 or higher, you are obese, and if your BMI is higher than 40, you are morbidly obese, and if the measure is higher than 50, you are super morbidly obese. My BMI is higher than 50.

In truth, many medical designations are arbitrary.

It is worth noting that in 1998, medical professionals, under the direction of the National Heart, Lung, and Blood Institute, lowered the BMI threshold for 'normal' bodies to below 25 and, in doing so, doubled the number of obese Americans. One of their reasons for lowering the cutoff: 'A round number like 25 would be easy for people to remember.'

These terms themselves are somewhat horrifying. 'Obese' is an unpleasant word from the Latin *obesus*, meaning 'having eaten until fat,' which is, in a literal sense, fair enough. But when people use the word 'obese,' they aren't merely being literal. They are offering forth an accusation. It is strange, and perhaps sad, that medical doctors came up with this terminology when they are charged with first doing no harm. The modifier 'morbidly' makes the fat body a death sentence when such is not the case. The term 'morbid obesity' frames fat people like we are the walking dead, and the medical establishment treats us accordingly.

The cultural measure for obesity often seems to be anyone who appears to be larger than a size 6, or anyone whose body doesn't naturally cater to the male gaze, or anyone with cellulite on her thighs.

I do not weigh 577 pounds now. I am still very fat, but I weigh about 150 pounds less than that. With every new diet attempt I shave off a few pounds here, a few pounds there. This is all relative. I am not small. I will never be small. For one, I am tall. That is both a curse and a saving grace. I have presence, I am told. I take up space. I intimidate. I do not want to take up space. I want to go unnoticed. I want to hide. I want to disappear until I gain control of my body.

I don't know how things got so out of control, or I do. This is my refrain. Losing control of my body was a matter of accretion. I began eating to change my body. I was willful in this. Some boys had destroyed me, and I barely survived it. I knew I wouldn't be able to endure another such violation, and so I ate because I thought that if my body became repulsive, I could keep men away. Even at that young age, I understood that to be fat was to be undesirable to men, to be beneath their contempt, and I already knew too much about their contempt. This is what most girls are taught – that we should be slender and small. We should not take up space. We should be seen and not heard, and if we are seen, we should be pleasing to men, acceptable to society. And most women know this, that we are supposed to disappear, but it's something that needs to be said, loudly, over and over again, so that we can resist surrendering to what is expected of us.

CHAPTER 5

What you need to know is that my life is split in two, cleaved not so neatly. There is the before and the after. Before I gained weight. After I gained weight. Before I was raped. After I was raped.

CHAPTER 6

In the before of my life, I was so very young and sheltered. I knew nothing about anything. I didn't know I could suffer or the breadth and scope of what suffering could be. I didn't know that I could give voice to my suffering when I did suffer. I didn't know there were better ways to deal with my suffering. Of all the things I wish I knew then that I know now, I wish I had known I could talk to my parents and get help, and turn to something other than food. I wish I had known that my violation was not my fault.

What I did know was food, so I ate because I understood that I could take up more space. I could become more solid, stronger, safer. I understood, from the way I saw people stare at fat people, from the way I stared at fat people, that too much weight was undesirable. If I was undesirable, I could keep more hurt away. At least, I hoped I could keep more hurt away because in the after, I knew too much about hurt. I knew too much about hurt, but I didn't know how much more a girl could suffer until I did.

But. This is what I did. This is the body I made. I am corpulent – rolls of brown flesh, arms and thighs and belly. The fat eventually had nowhere to go, so it created its own paths around my body. I am riven with stretch marks, pockets of cellulite on my massive thighs. The fat created a new body, one that shamed me but one that made me feel safe, and more than anything, I desperately needed to feel safe. I needed to feel like a fortress, impermeable. I did not want anything or anyone to touch me.

I did this to myself. This is my fault and my responsibility. This is what I tell myself, though I should not bear the responsibility for this body alone.

CHAPTER 7

This is the reality of living in my body: I am trapped in a cage. The frustrating thing about cages is that you're trapped but you can see exactly what you want. You can reach out from the cage, but only so far.

It would be easy to pretend I am just fine with my body as it is. I wish I did not see my body as something for which I should apologize or provide explanation. I'm a feminist and I believe in doing away with the rigid beauty standards that force women to conform to unrealistic ideals. I believe we should have broader definitions of beauty that include diverse body types. I believe it is so important for women to feel comfortable in their bodies, without wanting to change every single thing about their bodies to find that comfort. I (want to) believe my worth as a human being does not reside in my size or appearance. I know, having grown up in a culture that is generally toxic to women and constantly trying to discipline women's bodies, that it is important to resist unreasonable standards for how my body or any body should look.

What I know and what I feel are two very different things.

Feeling comfortable in my body isn't entirely about beauty standards. It is not entirely about ideals. It's about how I feel in my skin and bones, from one day to the next.

I am not comfortable in my body. Nearly everything physical is difficult. When I move around, I feel every extra pound I am carrying. I have no stamina. When I walk for long periods of time, my thighs and calves ache. My feet ache. My lower back aches. More often than not, I am in some kind of physical pain. Every morning, I am so stiff I contemplate just spending the duration of the day in bed. I have a pinched nerve, and so if I stand for too long, my right leg goes numb and then I sort of lurch about until the feeling returns.

When it's hot, I sweat profusely, mostly from my head, and then I feel self-conscious and find myself constantly wiping the sweat from my face. Rivulets of sweat spring forth between my breasts and pool at the base of my spine. My shirt gets damp and sweat stains begin seeping through the fabric. I feel like people are staring at me sweating and judging me for having an unruly body that perspires so wantonly, that dares to reveal the costs of its exertion.

There are things I want to do with my body but cannot. If I am with friends, I cannot keep up, so I am constantly thinking up excuses to explain why I am walking slower than they are, as if they don't already know. Sometimes, they pretend not to know, and sometimes, it seems like they are genuinely that oblivious to how different bodies move and take up space as they look back at me and suggest we do impossible things like go to an amusement park or walk a mile up a hill to a stadium or go hiking to an overlook with a great view.

My body is a cage. My body is a cage of my own making. I am still trying to figure my way out of it. I have been trying to figure a way out of it for more than twenty years.

CHAPTER 8

In writing about my body, maybe I should study this flesh, the abundance of it, as a crime scene. I should examine this corporeal effect to determine the cause.

I don't want to think of my body as a crime scene. I don't want to think of my body as something gone horribly wrong, something that should be cordoned off and investigated.

Is my body a crime scene when I already know I am the perpetrator, or at least one of the perpetrators?

Or should I see myself as the victim of the crime that took place in my body?

I am marked, in so many ways, by what I went through. I survived it, but that isn't the whole of the story. Over the years, I have learned the importance of survival and claiming the label of 'survivor,' but I don't mind the label of 'victim.' I also don't think there's any shame in saying that when I was raped, I became a victim, and to this day, while I am also many other things, I am still a victim.

It took me a long time, but I prefer 'victim' to

'survivor' now. I don't want to diminish the gravity of what happened. I don't want to pretend I'm on some triumphant, uplifting journey. I don't want to pretend that everything is okay. I'm living with what happened, moving forward without forgetting, moving forward without pretending I am unscarred.

This is the memoir of my body. My body was broken. I was broken. I did not know how to put myself back together. I was splintered. A part of me was dead. A part of me was mute and would stay that way for many years.

I was hollowed out. I was determined to fill the void, and food was what I used to build a shield around what little was left of me. I ate and ate and ate in the hopes that if I made myself big, my body would be safe. I buried the girl I had been because she ran into all kinds of trouble. I tried to erase every memory of her, but she is still there, somewhere. She is still small and scared and ashamed, and perhaps I am writing my way back to her, trying to tell her everything she needs to hear.

CHAPTER 9

I was broken, and to numb the pain of that brokenness, I ate and ate and ate, and then I was not just overweight or fat. Less than a decade later, I was morbidly obese and then I was super morbidly obese. I was trapped in my body, one I made but barely recognized or understood. I was miserable, but I was safe. Or at least I could tell myself I was safe.

My memories of the after are scattered, fragmentary, but I do clearly remember eating and eating and eating so I could forget, so my body could become so big it would never be broken again. I remember the quiet comfort of eating when I was lonely or sad or even happy.

Today, I am a fat woman. I don't think I am ugly. I don't hate myself in the way society would have me hate myself, but I do live in the world. I live in this body in this world, and I hate how the world all too often responds to this body. Intellectually, I recognize that I am not the problem. This world and its unwillingness to accept and accommodate me are the problem. But I suspect it is more likely that I can change before this culture and its attitudes toward fat people will change. In addition to fighting the 'good fight' about body positivity, I also need to think about the quality of my life in the here and now.

I have been living in this unruly body for more than twenty years. I have tried to make peace with this body. I have tried to love or at least tolerate this body in a world that displays nothing but contempt for it. I have tried to move on from the trauma that compelled me to create this body. I have tried to love and be loved. I have been silent about my story in a world where people assume they know the why of my body, or any fat body. And now, I am choosing to no longer be silent. I am tracing the story of my body from when I was a carefree young girl who could trust her body and who felt safe in her body, to the moment when that safety was destroyed, to the aftermath that continues even as I try to undo so much of what was done to me.

PART II

CHAPTER 10

There is a picture of me. My older cousin is holding me the weekend of my christening. I am still an infant, wearing a long white satin gown. We are sitting on a plastic-covered couch in New York City. In the picture my cousin is older, maybe five or six. I am squirming with senseless baby rage, my limbs at awkward angles.

I am grateful that there are so many pictures of me from my childhood because there is so much I have forgotten in one way or another.

There are years and years of my life I can't remember a thing about. A family member will say, 'Remember the time [insert significant family moment],' and I stare blankly, with no recollection of these moments whatsoever. We have a shared history and yet we do not. In many ways, that's the best means of describing my relationship with my family, and with nearly everyone in my life. There is the great life we share and the more difficult parts of my life we do not, that they know little about. There is no rhyme or reason to what I can and cannot remember. It's also hard to explain this absence of memory because there are moments from my childhood I remember like they were yesterday.

I have a good memory. I can remember conversations with friends almost word for word, even years after they occur. I remember how platinum blond the hair of my fourth grade teacher was or how I got in trouble for reading in class in the third grade because I was bored. I remember my aunt and uncle's wedding in Port-au-Prince and how my knee swelled like an orange after I was bitten by a mosquito. I remember good things. I remember bad things. When I have to, though, I can strip my memory bare, and I have done this, at times, when erasure was necessary.

I have photo albums taken from my parents' house, albums swollen with fading pictures of my two brothers and me when we were very young. This was before the digital age, and still, it seems like almost every moment of my life was photographed, and then each picture was developed and meticulously archived. Each album has a big number on it with a circle around that number. In many of the albums there are brief notes with names, ages, places. It's as if my mother knew these memories needed to be preserved for a reason. She raised my brothers and me with iron will and her own kind of grace. The fierceness of her love for and devotion to us is overwhelming, and this fierceness only grows stronger the older we get. When I was a child, my mother kept these albums in a neat, sequential row, and when one album was filled, she went and bought another album and filled it too.

My mother has tried to fill in some of the blanks from my childhood even if she doesn't realize she's doing it. She remembers everything, or that's how it seems, or that's how it was until I went away to boarding school, at thirteen, and then there was no one there to hold on to my memories for me.

My mom still takes pictures of everything and has more than twenty thousand pictures on her Flickr stream, pictures of her life and our lives and the people and places in our lives. At my doctoral defense, there she was, staring at me so proudly, every few minutes picking up her camera to snap a new picture, to capture every possible second of my moment. At a reading for my novel in New York City, there she was again with her camera, taking pictures, documenting another memorable moment.

People often notice that I take pictures of every little thing. I say I do it so I won't forget, so I cannot forget, all the amazing things I see and experience. I don't explain that memories matter more to me now that my life looks different. But it's more than that. The ways in which I am my mother's daughter are infinite.

The cover of my baby album is white with specks of glitter throughout. 'It's a girl!' is emblazoned across the cover. On the first page of this album are my parents' names, my date of birth, my height and weight, hair and eye color. There are two black imprints of my baby feet with the words 'Girl Gay' written above them. I was born at 7:48 in the morning, which is why, I am certain, I am not a morning person. There are blank lines for 'exciting memories in baby's life,' and all of those lines have been filled with my first tiny accomplishments. Apparently I read the alphabet at two and a half years old and could tell time at three. My mother proudly wrote, 'Reads almost everything at five years old.' Those are her exact words, written in her neat penmanship, though family lore has me reading the newspaper with my dad about a year and a half before that.

For the first five years of my life, my mother recorded my height and weight. I had a big head that was triangular, something that can happen with the firstborn child. My mother says she spent hours smoothing my newborn head into a rounder shape. There was a record of my birth in the *Omaha World-Herald*, printed on October 28, 1974, thirteen days after my birthday, and the clipped section of the newspaper is stored in this album alongside my original birth certificate and the little card they put on my bassinet in the hospital. My mother was twenty-five and my father was twenty-seven, so young, but, given the era, not as young as many people were when they started families. My name is spelled correctly on my birth certificate, with one *n*, and the birth certificate is pink. A nuanced cultural understanding of gender did not exist then – girls were pink and boys were blue and that was that.

In the very first picture of my mother and me together, she is holding me and her jet-black hair is cascading down her back in a thick ponytail. She looks impossibly young and beautiful. I am three days old. This is actually not the first picture of us together. There is a picture of my mom, hugely pregnant with me, wearing a sassy blue minidress and a pair of chunky heels. Her hair is wild and hanging loose down her back. She is leaning against a car, giving a look to the photographer, my father, the kind of intimate look that makes me want to turn away to afford them some privacy. She put this picture in the album even though she is one of the most private people I know. She wanted me to see this gorgeous image, to know she and my father have always loved each other.

These oldest pictures have been in the album so long that they are stuck to the pages. To try and remove the pictures would ruin them.

Every picture of me as an infant with my parents reveals them smiling at me like I am the center of their world. I was. I am. This is part of my truth I know with real clarity – everything good and strong about me starts with my parents, absolutely everything. Almost every picture of me as an infant shows me smiling a smile so infectious that when I look at them I cannot help but smile too. There are happy babies and there are happy babies. I was a happy baby. This is indisputable.

Babies are cute, but they're pretty useless, my best friend says. They can't do much for themselves. You have to love them through that uselessness. In the pictures where I am alone, I am being propped up by the arm of a chair, or a few pillows. In one picture, on a hideous, thickly brocaded red couch, I am alone and visibly screaming my head off. There is more than one picture of me screaming my head off. Pictures of screaming babies are hilarious when you know they are pictures of happy babies who are simply having a random fit of baby rage. I look at these baby pictures and think, *I look like my niece*, but really it is my young niece who looks like me. Family is powerful, no matter what. We're always tied together with our eyes and our lips and our blood and our bloody hearts. When I was three, my brother Joel was born. There are pictures of him, brown and round, a full head of hair, sitting or standing next to me.

As an adult, I have gone through these albums many times. I have been trying to remember. At first, I looked for pictures to show a child of my own, 'This is where you come from,' so when I have that child, she might know her family knows how to love, however imperfectly, so she knows her mother has always been loved and so she may know that she, in turn, will always be loved. It is important to show a child love in many forms, and this is the one good thing I have to offer, no matter how this child comes into my life. I also study the pictures, the people in them; I recall the names and places, the moments that matter, so many of which elude me. I try to piece together the memories I have so carefully erased. I try to make sense of how I went from the child in these perfect photographed moments to who I am today.

I know, precisely, and yet I do not know. I know, but I think what I really want is to understand the why of the distance between then and now. The why is complicated and slippery. I want to be able to hold the why in my hands, to dissect it or tear it apart or burn it and read the ashes even though I am afraid of what I will do with what I see there. I don't know if such understanding is possible, but when I am alone, I sit and slowly page through these albums obsessively. I want to see what is there and what is missing and what happened even if the why still eludes me.

There is a picture of me. I am five. I have big eyes and a scrawny neck. I am staring at a plastic typewriter while I lie on a couch, on my stomach, ankles crossed, probably daydreaming. I always daydreamed. Even then, I was a writer. From an early age, I would draw little villages on napkins and write stories about the people who lived in those villages. I loved the escape of writing those stories, of imagining lives that were different from my own. I had a ferocious imagination. I was a daydreamer and I resented being pulled out of my daydreams to deal with the business of living. In my stories, I could write myself the friends I did not have. I could make so many things possible that I did not dare imagine for myself. I could be brave. I could be smart. I could be funny. I could be everything I ever wanted. When I wrote, it was so easy to be happy.

There is a picture of me. I am seven; I am happy, wearing overalls. I wore overalls a lot as a kid. I liked them for lots of reasons, but mostly I liked them because they had many pockets where I could hide things and because they were complicated and had lots of buttons and things requiring fastening. They made me feel safe, cozy. In probably one out of every three or four pictures from that period, I am wearing overalls. That's strange, but I was strange. In this particular picture, I am with my brother Joel and he is karate kicking me as I try to avoid his little foot. He was and is very energetic. We are three years apart. We are having fun. We are still very close. We were cute kids. It kills me to see that kind of naked joy in myself. I would give almost anything to be that free again.

When I was eight, my brother Michael Jr was born, and then there were three of us in all the pictures, often huddled together, or holding hands as we stared into the camera.

As much as I wrote, I lost myself in books even more. I read everything I could get my hands on. My favorite books were the *Little House on the Prairie* books. I loved the idea that Laura Ingalls, an ordinary girl from the plains, could live an ordinary extraordinary life in a time so different from mine. I loved all the details in the books – Pa bringing home delectable oranges, making candy in the snow with maple syrup, the bond shared by the Ingalls sisters, Laura being called half-pint. As the Ingalls girls grew up, I loved Laura's rivalry with Nellie Oleson and her court-ship with Almanzo Wilder, who would eventually become her husband. I was breathless when I read about the first years of their marriage as home-steaders, enduring the trials of farming and raising their daughter, Rose. I wanted that kind of steady, true love for myself, and I wanted a relationship where I could be independent but loved and looked after at the same time.

When I moved on from *Little House on the Prairie*, I read everything by Judy Blume. I mostly learned about sex from her novel *Forever* . . ., and for many years, I assumed that all men called their dicks 'Ralph.' I read books about adven-turous girls mining for gold in California and surviving the trials and tribulations of the wagon trail. I became intensely obsessed with the loving rivalry of Jessica and Elizabeth Wakefield in the idyllic California town of Sweet Valley. I read *Clan of the Cave Bear* and learned that sex could be far more interesting than the youthful fumblings of Katherine and Michael in *Forever* . . . had indi-cated. I read and read and read. My imagination expanded infinitely.

There are countless pictures of me wearing skirts and dresses, pictures where I am a girly girl with long, done-up hair, jewelry, doing the whole pretty-princess thing. I long thought I was a tomboy because I was the only girl in my family. Sometimes we try to convince ourselves of things that are not true, reframing the past to better explain the present. When I look at these pictures, it is quite clear that while I enjoyed roughhousing and playing in dirt with my brothers and such, I wasn't entirely a tomboy, not really.

I played with G.I. Joe action figures and built forts in the empty lot next to our home and caroused in the woods on the edge of our neighborhood because my brothers were my playmates. Most of the time, my brothers were my best friends besides the ones I found in books. The three of us got along well, except when we bickered, and oh, we could bicker, particularly my brother Joel and me. We bickered about everything and nothing and then we made up and made trouble. The baby, Michael Jr, was so much younger that he was, generally, a willing accomplice to our shenanigans. When he wasn't our accomplice, he was the target of petty cruelties, like when we sent him down the basement stairs in a laundry basket or tormented him with a plastic spider or, worst of all, ignored his plaintive desire to play with us. Somehow, through it all, he adored us, and Joel and I basked in the glow of his adoration.

These pictures from the photo albums of my

childhood are artifacts of a time when I was happy and whole. They are evidence that, once, I was pretty and sometimes sweet. Beneath what you see now, there is still a pretty girl who loves pretty-girl things.

In these pictures, I get older. I smile less. I am still pretty. When I am twelve, I stop wearing skirts or most jewelry or doing anything with my hair, instead wearing it back in a tight bun or ponytail. I am still pretty. A few years after that, I will cut most of my hair off and start wearing oversized men's clothing. I am less pretty. In these pictures I stare at the camera. I look hollow. I am hollow.

CHAPTER 11

I don't know how to talk about rape and sexual violence when it comes to my own story. It is easier to say, 'Something terrible happened.'

Something terrible happened. That something terrible broke me. I wish I could leave it at that, but this is a memoir of my body so I need to tell you what happened to my body. I was young and I took my body for granted and then I learned about the terrible things that could happen to a girl body and everything changed.

Something terrible happened, and I wish I could leave it at that because as a writer who is also a woman, I don't want to be defined by the worst thing that has happened to me. I don't want my personality to be consumed in that way. I don't want my work to be consumed or defined by this terrible something.

At the same time, I don't want to be silent. I can't be silent. I don't want to pretend nothing terrible has ever happened to me. I don't want to carry all the secrets I carried, alone, for too many years. I cannot do these things anymore.

If I must share my story, I want to do so on my

terms, without the attention that inevitably follows. I do not want pity or appreciation or advice. I am not brave or heroic. I am not strong. I am not special. I am one woman who has experienced something countless women have experienced. I am a victim who survived. It could have been worse, so much worse. That's what matters and is even more a travesty here, that having this kind of story is utterly common. I hope that by sharing my story, by joining a chorus of women and men who share their stories too, more people can become appropriately horrified by how much suffering is born of sexual violence, how far-reaching the repercussions can be.

I often write around what happened to me because that is easier than going back to that day, to everything leading up to that day, to what happened after. It's easier than facing myself and the ways, despite everything I know, in which I feel culpable for what happened. Even now, I feel guilt not only for what happened, but for how I handled the after, for my silence, for my eating and what became of my body. I write around what happened because I don't want to have to defend myself. I don't want to have to deal with the horror of such exposure. I guess that makes me a coward, afraid, weak, human.

I write around what happened because I don't want my family to have these terrible images in their heads. I don't want them to know what I endured and then kept secret for more than twenty-five years. I don't want my lover seeing only a moment from my assault when they look at me. I don't want them to think me more fragile than I am. I am stronger than I am broken. I don't want them, or anyone, to think I am nothing more than the worst thing that has ever happened to me. I want to protect the people I love. I want to protect myself. My story is mine, and on most days, I wish I could bury that story, somewhere deep where I might be free of it. But. It has been thirty years and, inexplicably, I am still not free of it.

I all too often write around my story, but still, I write. I share parts of my story, and this sharing becomes part of something bigger, a collective testimony of people who have painful stories too. I make that choice.

We don't necessarily know how to hear stories about any kind of violence, because it is hard to accept that violence is as simple as it is complicated, that you can love someone who hurts you, that you can stay with someone who hurts you, that you can be hurt by someone who loves you, that you can be hurt by a complete stranger, that you can be hurt in so many terrible, intimate ways.

I also share what I do of my story because I believe in the importance of sharing histories of violence. I am reticent to share my own history of violence, but that history informs so much of who I am, what I write, how I write. It informs how I move through the world. It informs how I love and allow myself to be loved. It informs everything.

It is easier to use detached language like 'assault' or 'violation' or 'incident' than it is to come out and say that when I was twelve years old, I was gang-raped by a boy I thought I loved and a group of his friends.

When I was twelve years old, I was raped.

So many years past being raped, I tell myself what happened is 'in the past.' This is only partly true. In too many ways, the past is still with me. The past is written on my body. I carry it every single day. The past sometimes feels like it might kill me. It is a very heavy burden.

In my history of violence, there was a boy. I loved him. His name was Christopher. That's not really his name. You know that. I was raped by Christopher and several of his friends in an abandoned hunting cabin in the woods where no one but those boys could hear me scream.

Before that, though, Christopher and I were friends or at least shared a semblance of friendship. During school hours, he would ignore me, but after school we would hang out. We would do whatever he wanted. He was always in control of the time we spent together. In truth, he treated me terribly and I thought I should be grateful that he bothered to treat me terribly, that he bothered with a girl like me at all. I had no reason to have such low self-esteem at twelve years old. I had no reason to allow myself to be treated terribly. It happened anyway. That gnawing truth is a lot of what I still struggle to free myself from.

This boy and I were riding bikes in the woods when we stopped at the cabin, this disgusting, forgotten place where teenagers got up to no good. His friends were waiting and then we were standing inside the cabin and Christopher was bragging to them about things he and I had done, private things, and I was so embarrassed because I was a good Catholic girl and I already felt so very guilty that Christopher and I had done things we should not have done.

I was confused because I had no idea why he would tell his friends what I had never told anyone, what I thought was our secret, what made him love me or at least keep me around. His friends were excited by the things Christopher said. They were so very excited, their faces flushed and their laughs raucous. While they talked around me, I felt smaller and smaller. I was scared even if I couldn't recognize the strange energy running through me.

I did try to run out of there once I realized I was not safe, but it was no use. I could not save myself.

Christopher pushed me down in front of his laughing friends, so many bodies larger than mine. I was so scared and embarrassed and confused. I was hurt because I loved him and thought he loved me, and in a matter of moments, there I was, splayed out in front of his friends. I wasn't a girl to them. I was a thing, flesh and girl bones with which they could amuse themselves. When Christopher lay on top of me, he didn't take off his clothes. This detail stays with me, that he had such little regard for what he was about to do to me. He just unzipped his jeans and knelt between my legs and shoved himself inside of me. Those other boys stared down at me, leered really, and egged Christopher on. I closed my eyes because I did not want to see them. I did not want to accept what was happening. As a sheltered, *good* Catholic girl, I barely understood what was happening. I did understand the pain, though, the sharpness and the immediacy of it. That pain was inescapable and held me in my body when I wanted to abandon it to those boys and hide myself somewhere safe.

I begged Christopher to stop. I told him I would do anything he wanted if he would just make it all stop, but he didn't stop. He didn't look at me. Christopher took a long time or at least it felt like a long time because I did not want him inside me. It did not matter what I wanted.

After Christopher came, he switched places with the boy who was holding my arms down. I fought, but my fighting didn't do much more than make those boys laugh. The friend held me down, his lips shiny, his beer breath in my face. To this day, I cannot stand beer breath. I thought I would break beneath the weight of those boys.

I was already so sore. Christopher refused to

look at me. He just held my wrists, spat on my face. I told myself, I still tell myself, he was just trying to impress his friends. I tell myself he didn't mean it. He laughed. All those boys raped me. They tried to see how far they could go. I was a toy, used recklessly. Eventually, I stopped screaming, I stopped moving, I stopped fighting. I stopped praying and believing God would save me. I did not stop hurting. The pain was constant. They took a break. I huddled into myself and shook. I couldn't move. I could not believe what was happening. I literally had no capacity for understanding my story as it was being written.

I don't remember their names. Other than Christopher, I don't remember distinct details about them. They were boys who were not yet men but knew, already, how to do the damage of men. I remember their smells, the squareness of their faces, the weight of their bodies, the tangy smell of their sweat, the surprising strength in their limbs. I remember that they enjoyed themselves, and laughed a lot. I remember that they had nothing but disdain for me.

They did things I've never been able to talk about, and will never be able to talk about. I don't know how. I don't want to find those words. I have a history of violence, but the public record of it will always be incomplete.

When it was all over, I pushed my bike home and I pretended to be the daughter my parents knew, the good girl, the straight-A student. I don't know how I hid what happened, but I knew how to be a good girl, and I guess I played that part exceptionally well that night.

Later, those boys told everyone at school what happened or, rather, a version of the story that made my name 'Slut' for the rest of the school year. I immediately understood that my version of the story would never matter, so I kept the truth of what happened a secret and tried to live with this new name.

He said/she said is why so many victims (or survivors, if you prefer that terminology) don't come forward. All too often, what 'he said' matters more, so we just swallow the truth. We swallow it, and more often than not, that truth turns rancid. It spreads through the body like an infection. It becomes depression or addiction or obsession or some other physical manifestation of the silence of what she would have said, needed to say, couldn't say.

With every day that went by, I hated myself more. I disgusted myself more. I couldn't get away from him. I couldn't get away from what those boys did. I could smell them and feel their mouths and their tongues and their hands and their rough bodies and their cruel skin. I couldn't stop hearing the terrible things they said to me. Their voices were with me, constantly. Hating myself became as natural as breathing.

Those boys treated me like nothing so I became nothing.

CHAPTER 12

There is a before and an after. In the after I was broken, shattered and silent. I was numb. I was terrified. I carried this secret and knew, in my soul, that what those boys did to me had to stay secret. I couldn't share the shame and humiliation of it. I was disgusting because I had allowed disgusting things to be done to me. I was not a girl. I was less than human. I was no longer a good girl and I was going to hell.

I was twelve, and suddenly, I was no longer a child. I no longer felt free or happy or safe. I became more and more withdrawn. If I had a saving grace, it was that we moved all the time for my father's job, and the summer after I was raped we moved to a new state where I could have my name again and no one knew I was the girl in the woods. I still had no friends and I did not try to make friends, because how could we possibly have anything in common? I did not dare subject what I had become to the children around me. I read, obsessively. When I read on the school bus, my classmates teased me. Sometimes, they took my book from me and threw it back and forth as I flailed, helplessly, just trying to get that book back into my hands. When I read, I could forget. I could be anywhere in the world except in the eighth grade, lonely and holding tightly to my secret. I often say that reading and writing saved my life. I mean that quite literally.

At home, I tried to be the good girl my parents thought me to be, but it was exhausting. On so many occasions, I wanted to tell them something was wrong, that I was dying inside, but I couldn't find the words. I couldn't find a way to overcome my fear of what they might say and do and think of me. The longer I stayed silent, the more that fear grew until it dwarfed everything else.

I couldn't let my parents see who or what I had become because they would be disgusted and they would discard me like the trash I knew myself to be, and then I would not only be nothing, I would have nothing. There was no room in my life for the truth.

I know, now, that I was wrong, that my parents would have supported me, helped me, and sought justice for me. They would have shown me that the shame was not mine to bear. Unfortunately, my fearful silence cannot be undone. I cannot tell that twelve-year-old girl who was so scared and alone just how much she was loved, how uncon-ditionally, but oh, how I want to. How I want to comfort her. How I want to save her from so much of what would happen next.

I played the part of good girl, good daughter,

good student. I went to church even though I had no faith. Guilt consumed me. I no longer believed in God because surely if there were a God, he would have saved me from Christopher and those boys in the woods. I no longer believed in God because I had sinned. I had sinned in a way I hadn't even known was possible until I learned what was possible. It was lonely and terrifying to be unmoored from everything that had been so important in my life – my family, my faith, myself.

I was alone with my secret, pretending to be a different kind of girl. To survive, I tried to forget what had happened, those boys, the stink of their breath, their hands taking my body from me, killing me from the inside out.

CHAPTER 13

Before this terrible thing happened, I had already started to lose my body. I was too young, in a sad semblance of a relationship with a boy who knew too much, wanted too much. I wanted too much too, but he and I wanted very different things. Christopher wanted to use me. I wanted him to love me. I wanted him to fill the loneliness, to ease the ache of being awkward, of being the girl always on the outside looking in. When I met him, we had just moved to the area.

I had (and have?) this void, this cavern of loneliness inside me that I have spent my whole life trying to fill. I was willing to do most anything if that boy would ease my loneliness. I wanted to feel like he and I belonged to each other, but each time we were together and then after, I felt quite the opposite. And still, I was drawn to him.

At the time I was, and would continue to be for many years, obsessed with the *Sweet Valley High* books. I read them voraciously because I was nothing like Elizabeth and Jessica Wakefield or even Enid Rollins. I would never date a boy like Todd Wilkins, the handsome captain of the basketball team, or Bruce Patman, the handsome, wealthy bad boy of Sweet Valley. When I read the books, though, I could pretend that a better life was possible for me, one where I fit in somewhere, anywhere, and I had friends and a handsome boyfriend and a loving family who knew everything about me. In a better life, I could pretend I was a good girl.

This boy Christopher, so handsome and so popular, was my piece of Sweet Valley High in my well-manicured, suburban neighborhood. Certainly, no one could know this because he never acknowledged me at school, but I knew and I told myself that was enough. For many, many years to come, I would keep telling myself that the barest minimum of acknowledgment from lovers was enough.

We would hang out in his bedroom and flip through worn copies of his older brother's *Playboy* and *Hustler* magazines. I studied these naked women, mostly young white blond thin taut. Their bodies seemed alien, unreal. I knew it was wrong to look at these women displaying such wanton nakedness, but I couldn't look away.

He clearly found these women exciting, sexually attractive, and I knew, even then, that I was nothing like them. I didn't really want to be like those women but I wanted him to want me and I wanted him to look at me the way he looked at the magazines. He never did, and in his way, he punished me for what I wasn't and couldn't be.

He punished me for being too young and too naïve, too adoring and too accommodating.

I was a thing to him, even before he and his friends raped me. He wanted to try things and I was extraordinarily pliable. I didn't know how to say no. It never crossed my mind to say no. This was the price I had to pay, I told myself, to be loved by him or, if I was honest with myself, to be tolerated by him. A girl like me, pliable and sheltered and unworthy and desperately craving his attention, did not dare hope for anything more. I knew that.

I cannot bring myself to detail the things he did to me before I was broken. It's too much, too humiliating. But with each new transgression we committed, I lost more of my body. I fell further from the possibility of the word 'no.' I became less and less the good girl I had been. I stopped looking at my reflection in the mirror because I felt nothing but guilt and shame when I did.

And then there was that terrible day in the woods. And I finally did say no. And it did not matter. That's what has scarred me the most. My no did not matter. I wish I could tell you I never spoke to Christopher again, but I did. That may be what shames me most, that after everything he did to me, I went back, and allowed him to continue using me until my family moved a few months later. I allowed him to continue using me because I didn't know what else to do. Or I let him use me because after what happened in the woods, I felt so worthless. I believed I didn't deserve any better.

I was marked after that. Men could smell it on me, that I had lost my body, that they could avail themselves of my body, that I wouldn't say no because I knew my no did not matter. They smelled it on me and took advantage, every chance they got.

CHAPTER 14

I do not know why I turned to food. Or I do. I was lonely and scared and food offered an immediate satisfaction. Food offered comfort when I needed to be comforted and did not know how to ask for what I needed from those who loved me. Food tasted good and made me feel better. Food was the one thing within my reach.

Until I started gaining weight, I had a healthy attitude toward food. My mother is not a woman with a passion for cooking, but she harbors an intense passion for her family. Throughout my childhood, she prepared healthy, well-rounded meals for us, which we ate together at the dinner table. There were no rushed dinners sitting in front of the television or standing at the kitchen counter. We kids eagerly talked about our latest school projects, like a suspension bridge made out of balsa wood or a baking soda volcano. We shared our accomplishments, like a good report card – which was of course the expectation – or a goal scored in a soccer match. My brothers and I bickered toward the end of dinner, usually over who would do the dishes. My parents, Haitian immigrants, talked about things we only half understood, like the *American* neighbors or my father's latest construction project. We talked about the goings-on of the world. We talked about what we wanted for ourselves. I took it for granted that this is what all families did – come together and become an island unto themselves, the kitchen table the sun around which we revolved.

The food my mother cooked for us was good, but it was secondary to the way we invested in being so connected to one another. My parents always made it seem like my brothers and I were terribly interesting, asking us thoughtful questions about our childish musings, urging us to be our best selves. If we were slighted, they were offended on our behalf. When we had some small moment of glory, they reveled in it. I fell asleep most nights flush with the joy of knowing I belonged to these people and they belonged to me.

Even as I became more and more withdrawn, my family remained strong, connected in these intimate, indelible ways. I have no doubt that my parents noticed the change in me. They would continue to notice, to worry over me, for the next twenty years and longer. But they didn't know how to talk to me and I didn't let them in. When they tried, I deflected, refusing to take the lifelines they offered me. The longer I kept my secret, the more attached I became to keeping my truth to myself, the more I nurtured my silence.

CHAPTER 15

The only way I know of moving through the world is as a Haitian American, a Haitian daughter. A Haitian daughter is a good girl. She is respectful, studious, hard-working. She never forgets the importance of her heritage. We are part of the first free black nation in the Western Hemisphere, my brothers and I were often told. No matter how far we have fallen, when it matters most, we rise.

Haitians love the food from our island, but they judge gluttony. I suspect this rises out of the poverty for which Haiti is too often and too narrowly known. When you are overweight in a Haitian family, your body is a family concern. Everyone – siblings, parents, aunts, uncles, grand-mothers, cousins – has an opinion, judgment, or piece of counsel. They mean well. We love hard and that love is inescapable. My family has been inordinately preoccupied with my body since I was thirteen years old.

My mother, who stayed home to raise my brothers and me, did not teach me how to cook, and I had little interest in being taught. I just enjoyed watching her prepare our meals from the periphery of the kitchen – the efficiency with which she pursued the task always impressed me. Her brow furrowed in concentration. She could hold a conversation, but when something demanded her attention, she hushed and it was like the whole world fell away from her. She did not enjoy sharing the kitchen space and did not want help. She always wore latex gloves, like a doctor – to avoid contamination, she said. She was known to add a drop of Clorox to the water when washing meat or fruit or vegetables. She washed a dish or cutting board or bowl immediately after it had been used. Save for the aromas wafting from the gas stove, you would never know my mother was cooking.

Throughout my childhood, my mother prepared a bewildering combination of foods – American dishes from the *Betty Crocker Cookbook* or *The Joy of Cooking* one night, and a Haitian meal the next. The dishes I remember, the ones I love most, are Haitian – legumes, fried plantains, red rice, black rice; *griyo*, or pork marinated in blood orange and roasted with shallots; Haitian macaroni and cheese – everything served with sauce (a tomato-based sauce with thyme, peppers, and onions) and spicy pickled vegetables, everything made from scratch. This was how my mother demonstrated her affection.

My mother didn't believe in processed foods or fast food, so I have never eaten many foods people take for granted – TV dinners, Chef Boyardee,

Kraft Mac & Cheese. She was ahead of her time. Her stance infuriated my brothers and me because our American friends got to eat magical foods like sugary breakfast cereals, and snack on Cheetos and Chips Ahoy and Little Debbie Snack Cakes. 'Fruit is a snack,' my mom would tell us. I vowed, when I grew up, to decorate my home with clear glass bowls filled with M&M's and she laughed.

The older we got, the laxer my mom became. By the time my youngest brother arrived, junk food had breached the perimeter of our home, though in the moderation entirely characteristic of my parents.

CHAPTER 16

At thirteen, I went to boarding school. We had moved around a lot throughout my childhood, following my father and his successful career as a civil engineer. He built tunnels – the Eisenhower Tunnel in Colorado; subway lines in New York and Washington, DC; an outfall project in Boston. When my brothers and I visited him on construction sites, my dad would secure hard hats on our heads and take us belowground, so deep and dark, and show us how he, quite literally, was changing the world.

His company was headquartered in Omaha, but whenever his district got a new project, he would be dispatched, and off we would go for a year or two – Illinois, Colorado, New Jersey, Virginia – and then back to Omaha we would return. I began exploring boarding schools so I might attend one school for all four years of high school. I was, I admit, also enamored with *The Girls of Canby Hall* series of books by Emily Chase. I would be like Shelley Hyde from Iowa, the fish out of water who still forged lifelong friendships with her new roommates as they had youthful adventures against the backdrop of their quintessentially New England campus.

And then I was raped and I had to pretend to be someone I wasn't and I wanted nothing more than to run away. Attending boarding school is how upper-middle-class girls run away, to be sure. If I went away for high school, I wouldn't have to pretend to be a good girl who knew nothing of the world. I could be the nothing I had become, without having to explain myself. I could continue clinging tightly, desperately, to my secret and my guilt and my shame.

Because I was so shy and withdrawn, because of all the moving around throughout my childhood, the only people I had to leave behind were my family. I didn't have any friends to miss. I didn't have a particular local high school I had been yearning to attend for years. I didn't even know where we would be living for my freshman year, if my dad was transferred again. I was only thirteen, but it was surprisingly easy to decide that I wanted to leave home.

I don't know what my parents noticed about me in the year before high school. Since we had moved, I no longer had to go to a school where everyone called me Slut. Instead, there were new torments, new bullies, and even more motivation for me to run, run, run as far away from myself as possible. I applied to several boarding schools and got into them all. One, Lawrenceville, accepted me as part of the first class of girls to attend the school when it went coed, but the thought of attending a school with so many boys was too much. I ended up going to Exeter because my cousin Claudine had just graduated from there and she seemed fine and the school seemed fine and because my parents liked the school's reputation. At such a young age, I absolutely took for granted that I would be attending one of the most elite and expensive high schools in the country, if not the world. All that mattered was that I would be able to run away.

Left to my own devices at boarding school, I lost any semblance of control over what I put into my body. Suddenly, there were all kinds of food available to me. The dining hall was an all-you-can-eat extravaganza. Certainly, the offerings were generally bad – damp and malodorous, as is the nature of industrially prepared food – but there were vast quantities available. And there was a salad bar. And there were peanut butter and jelly sandwiches. And breakfast cereal. And limitless soda machines. And dessert options. And The Grill, a campus greasy spoon where, for a few dollars, I could get a burger, French fries, and a frappé. And there was the convenience store downtown, where I could buy a huge submarine sandwich. And a Woolworth's with an actual lunch counter. I could order pizza, and within thirty minutes, it would be delivered to my dorm and I could eat the entire thing by myself and there was no one to stop me from my naked, shameless indulgence. The freedom of being able to eat, so extravagantly and without limit, offered me the only true pleasure I knew in high school.

I was presented with an orgy of food and I indulged in all of it. I reveled in eating whatever I wanted, whenever I wanted. I reveled in the steam of biting into a salty French fry and the slick hot ooze of melted cheese on a hot slice of pizza and the thick cold sweetness of a frappé. I craved that pleasure and indulged myself as often as I could.

I was swallowing my secrets and making my body expand and explode. I found ways to hide in plain sight, to keep feeding a hunger that could never be satisfied – the hunger to stop hurting. I made myself bigger. I made myself safer. I created a distinct boundary between myself and anyone who dared to approach me. I created a boundary between myself and my family. I became of them but not.

Being at boarding school was also something of a shock to my understanding of the world. I had grown up middle class and then upper middle class, but at Exeter, I encountered students who came from families who harbored generations of wealth, fame, and/or infamy – the children of political scions, Hollywood celebrities, and industrial dynasties. I thought I knew wealth until I went to boarding school, and then I learned what wealth truly looks like. I learned that there are people with so much money at their disposal they take lavish spending for granted and have no interest in those without the same privileges. I didn't feel inadequate. However lost I was, I knew I was loved and lucky. But I was overwhelmed by how cavalierly these wealthy peers moved through the world, and how much was available to them.

As I was a black student from a reasonably well-off family, and I was from Nebraska, of all places, the white students didn't quite know what to do with me. I was an anomaly, and I didn't fit their assumed narrative about blackness. They assumed that all black students came from impoverished backgrounds and lived in the inner city. They assumed all black students attended Exeter by the grace of financial aid and white benevolence. Most of the black students only grudgingly accepted me into their social circles because I didn't fit their assumed narrative about blackness, either. As a Haitian American, I didn't have the same cultural touchstones. There were few students with whom I had any kind of common ground. As a socially awkward, shy girl, my loneliness became even more pronounced. Food was not only comfort; food also became my friend because it was constant and I didn't need to be anything but myself when I ate.

When I went home for that first Thanksgiving holiday, my parents were shocked, as if I were unrecognizable, and maybe, to them, I was. They saw me plainly while looking right through me. I had gained at least thirty pounds in only two and a half months. Suddenly, I was very round, my cheeks and gut and thighs fleshy in ways they had never been. My clothes, the ones that did fit, strained at the seams. Though I didn't want to go, my parents took me to a doctor who charitably declared that I was blossoming when so much more was happening to my body. He didn't seem overly concerned, likely attributed my weight gain to being away from home for the first time. My parents had no idea what to do, but they were incredibly alarmed and immediately began to treat my body as something of a crisis. They tried to help me without realizing that this early weight gain was only the beginning of the problem my body would become. They had no idea at all about what created the problem. They knew nothing of my determination to keep making my body into what I needed it to be – a safe harbor rather than a small, weak vessel that betrayed me.

CHAPTER 17

During the first two years of high school, I ate and ate and ate and I became more and more lost. I started high school as nothing and then became less than nothing. I only had to pretend to be the girl I had been when I spoke to my parents on the phone or when I went home for breaks. The rest of the time, I didn't know who I was. Mostly, I was numb. I was awkward. I was trying to be a writer. I was trying to forget what happened to me. I was trying to stop feeling those boys on and in my skin, how they laughed at me, how they laughed as they ruined me.

I remember so little from high school, but in the past few years, as my profile as a writer has gotten more visible, I've started to hear from the kids I went to high school with and, oddly enough, they all remember me distinctly. They reach out via e-mail, or Facebook, or at events, and ask me, eagerly, if I remember them too. They share anecdotes that make me seem like I was interesting and not as unbearable as I remember myself. I don't know what to make of the memories of other people or how to reconcile their memories with mine. I do know that I developed a sharp tongue in high school. I was quiet, but I could cut someone with words when I put my mind to it.

In my free time, I wrote a lot, dark and violent stories about young girls being tormented by terrible boys and men. I couldn't tell anyone what had happened to me, so I wrote the same story a thousand different ways. It was soothing to give voice to what I could not say out loud. I lost my voice but I had words. One of my English teachers, Rex McGuinn, recognized something in my stories. He told me I was a writer and he told me to write every day. I realize, now, that being told to write every day is writing advice many teachers give, but I took Mr McGuinn very seriously, as if he were offering me sacred counsel, and I write every day, still.

The most important thing Mr McGuinn did for me, though, was to walk me over to the campus counseling center. He saw I needed help and took me to a place where I could get that help. I won't say I found solace or salvation at the counseling center because I didn't. I wasn't ready. The first few sessions with my counselor, who was a man, were terrifying. I sat on the edge of my seat, staring at the door, plotting all potential routes of escape. I did not want to be alone with any man, let alone with a stranger, in a room with a closed door. I knew what could happen. And still, I kept going back, maybe because Mr McGuinn asked me to, maybe because some part of me knew I needed help, and I was so hungry for it.

CHAPTER 18

I ate and ate and ate at school. At home for breaks, I made a show of dieting (and continued eating everything I really wanted to eat, in secret). This double life of eating would become something that stayed with me well into adulthood. It lingers even now. My parents tried to figure out why I was gaining so much weight. I had no answers I could share with them. They put me on a medically supervised liquid diet during the summer after my freshman year. Every day, I drank five milk shakes that were chalky and disgusting. Of course I lost weight – forty pounds, maybe more. My parents were pleased that I had gotten my body under control. I went back to school, and my classmates admired my new body, offered me compliments, wanted to hang out with me. That was the first time I realized that weight loss, thinness really, was social currency. Amidst this attention, I was losing my newfound invisibility, and it terrified me. I was scared of so much as a teenager.

Early in the first semester of my sophomore year, I lost what currency I had gained over the summer.

Within a few weeks, I immediately began eating again, working vigilantly to undo the progress I had made the previous summer. My newly narrowed face plumped up. My stomach strained against the waistbands of my pants. My breasts swelled wildly because not only was I gaining a lot of weight, I was going through puberty.

I still held on to the hope that my boarding school life might resemble *The Girls of Canby Hall*, that I would bond with all the girls in my dorm and all my teachers would love me. That was never my experience.

Loneliness remained a constant companion. I didn't have many friends. I was awkward and maladjusted around the friends I did have, and most of the time, I was certain they only tolerated me out of pity. I regularly said the wrong things. I invented a boyfriend, Mr X, and I don't know what makes me cringe more now – that I used this bizarre pseudonym for my invention or that I invented a pseudonym at all. I couldn't even come up with a credible name for the imaginary man of my dreams. Eventually, the girls in my social circle figured out that I'd described Mr X based on one of their boyfriends, which was, as you might imagine, incredibly awkward, and they did not let me forget it. I had no fashion sense. I didn't know how to style my hair. I didn't know how to be a normal girl. I didn't know how to be human. It was a sad, sad time. Every day was a crushing disappointment or gauntlet of humiliation.

And then, later in the fall of my sophomore year, I began experiencing severe pain in my abdomen. It would keep me up at night, gasping and in tears, alone in a dorm room, far from home. I went to the infirmary, which was not known for any kind of competence, and the staff asked me, over and over, if I might be pregnant. That was, in their minds, the most likely problem a teenage girl could have. I wasn't pregnant, but they weren't really interested in investigating further. They sent me on my way each time, not seeming to take me seriously. The medical community is not particularly interested in taking the pain of women seriously.

One night, I crawled to the door of the resident faculty member on my floor, a woman who, during my freshman year, had imitated me in a game of charades by widening her arms and waddling around the room until someone guessed my name as the clue. When she finally woke and came to the door, I was cold and sweating and clammy. Campus security took me to the local hospital, where the doctors discovered I had gallstones. I called my parents, terrified, and my dad told me not to worry. He told me to close my eyes and that in the morning, he would be there. I did as he said and when I woke up, there he was. That is the kind of father he has always been. I had emergency surgery, and my gallbladder was removed. It turned out the high-protein diet I had been on for the summer had not done my gallbladder any favors.

I spent about ten days in the infirmary, and ended up with a wicked new scar, tender to the touch.

During my recovery, I was still in pain, and before long, doctors discovered that the surgeon had left some gallstones inside me – such tiny objects causing so much pain. I was rushed to Mass General in Boston, my first ambulance ride, and I was scared again, but also excited in the way of a child who does not quite understand mortality. This time, both my parents came and fretted over me until I was better. Before long, I went back to school. I had lost weight with all the sickness, so once again, I had work to do to make my body bigger and bigger and bigger and safer.

CHAPTER 19

Though I mostly sat in the counselor's office silently and sullenly, I continued to go to therapy throughout high school. I didn't make a lot of progress, but it was a space where I could escape the pressure of needing to earn good grades at an aggressively demanding school. I could escape from being an unpopular and awkward teenager who was desperately lonely. I could escape from being a disappointing daughter.

Eventually, I was assigned to a woman counselor and she gave me a copy of *The Courage to Heal*, by Ellen Bass and Laura Davis. At first, I hated the book because it included a 'workbook,' as well as cheesy exercises I couldn't possibly take seriously. The language was too flowery and full of affirmations that also made me distrustful.

Many of the theories that book espouses have now been discredited, but at that time, when I was so scared and shattered, *The Courage to Heal* gave me a vocabulary for what I had been through. I needed that book as much as I hated it for all the infantile exercises it encouraged. I learned about victims and survivors and trauma, and that getting past trauma was possible. I learned that I was not alone. I learned that being raped wasn't my fault, and though I didn't believe everything I learned, it was important to know such ideas, such truths, were out there. I didn't feel like I was healing and I didn't feel like I could ever reshape myself into what that book suggested healing looked like, but I did feel like at least there was something of a map I could follow to get to a place where healing felt possible. I needed that solidarity and hope, even if I couldn't imagine a time when I would become whole again.

CHAPTER 20

There was one place where I could forget myself and my hurt – the theater department. In high school, I became a passionate drama geek, and fell in love with technical theater – all the backstage work that makes any given show possible. When I was working behind the scenes, my newfound girth didn't matter. My shyness didn't matter. I could be part of something without anyone in a show's audience knowing I was part of something.

The first show I ever worked on was *Little Shop of Horrors*, my freshman year. I worked in the sound booth, managing sound cues, and befriended Michael, the handsome young postgraduate student (or fifth-year senior) who manned the giant plant that comes out at the end of the show. At the end of the year, Michael would take me to his prom on a cruise around the Boston Harbor. He was so kind to me and never wanted anything from me but friendship. That was something of a revelation to me, that a young man could be kind.

As a theater geek, I learned how to build flats and paint the taut canvas to look like any backdrop or setting a show needed. I learned how to design sound effects and hang lights and endure the endless hours of a tech rehearsal. I wandered through the musty costume barn to find specific costume pieces and helped locate or create the props needed for a given show. When I was in the theater, all darkened and dusty, I was useful. I was competent. People told me to do things and I did those things. I could apply myself to the tasks at hand and forget about the boys in the woods and what they did to my body.

I got to watch plays and musicals brought to life. No matter the show, I loved the spectacle and the quirks of the actors who successfully pretended they were so much more than high school students. Our faculty members, Mrs Ogami-Sherwood and Mr Bateman, had big personalities and a passion for the theater. They held all of us drama geeks in their thrall. Mr Bateman was notorious for walking around with a tumbler filled with Diet Coke and vodka. He was balding, but what hair he did have was unruly, standing on edge. He favored black turtlenecks. Shortly after I graduated in 1992, he was convicted of possessing child pornography and sending that pornography across state lines. He was sentenced to five years in prison. Mrs Ogami-Sherwood had a thick head of long, curly hair. She was small in stature but tall in every other way. She tolerated no nonsense, and most of us were scared of her while yearning for her attention.

On show nights, I was often a stagehand. I would dress in all black and be part of the invisible machine that keeps a show running. I knew all the lines to any show I worked on, and with the other drama geeks who were as obsessed with theater as I was, we found a way to have a lot of fun and make a little magic. High school was terrible, but in the theater, we created, for one another, a place where we could fit in for a few hours at a time.

CHAPTER 21

Camp Kingsmont is a weight-loss and fitness camp that, when I attended, the summer after my sophomore year, was nestled in the picturesque Berkshires of Massachusetts. The brochure made everything look bucolic and inviting, so I knew, instantly, not to trust such propaganda. One summer during high school, my parents sent me to Kingsmont for several weeks – another attempt to solve the problem of my body. I did not have much say in the matter because they were determined to make me lose weight by any means necessary, and I had learned the lesson that saying no meant nothing, so it was off to camp I went.

I hate camping and the outdoors, and I especially hate the woods. The cabins where we campers stayed were rustic, at best, and located at the top of a rather steep hill we were forced to climb whenever we wanted to be in the cabin.

We didn't get to spend much time in our cabins, though, because the camp was aggressive about making us 'enjoy' the outdoors. The counselors kept us all busy with various activities designed to make us exercise without expressly feeling like we were exercising. At least, that was the conceit. I always felt like I was exercising. It was a nightmare – nature walks, swimming, organized sports, and, of course, the terrible treks up the hill after dinner and whenever I forgot something in my cabin. There were weigh-ins, and for three meals and a snack a day, we ate shitty nutritional food (lots of baked chicken and steamed broccoli and bland versions of normally delicious foods like pizza and hamburgers) designed to further promote weight loss. I distinctly remember an unnatural quantity of Jell-O being offered.

Again, I lost weight, but as one of the older campers, I also got to spend time with the counselors, most of whom were only three or four years older than us. At night, after the younger campers were put to bed, we would hang out around a fire pit behind one of the cabins. It was quietly thrilling to be included in a group in this small way, to feel like I was breaking the rules.

When I returned to my real life, home with my parents, I immediately abandoned all the other lessons I had learned and regained, once more, the weight I had lost, and then some. The enduring lesson I learned at Camp Kingsmont was how to smoke because the counselors let us bum cigarettes from them. Smoking was a habit I would lovingly nurture for eighteen years.

Smoking felt good and always gave me a light buzz. Smoking also made me feel cool when I knew I was very, very uncool. I loved the ceremony of smoking. Back then, I was very much into the performance of it. I bought a Zippo lighter, and always kept it filled with lighter fluid. I liked to flip it open and shut it against my thigh as a nervous tic.

I started with Virginia Slims, or Vagina Slimes as we called them, then moved on to Marlboro Reds, then Marlboro Lights, before finally settling on Camel Lights, hard pack, my cigarette of choice. Each time I got a new pack, I would tap the top of it against the palm of my hand several times to tamp the tobacco, then pull off the plastic wrap and the foil insert. I'd turn one cigarette upside down and then pull out another to smoke. I am sure I learned this little ritual from one of the camp counselors.

I loved smoking after a meal, first thing in the morning, right before bed. In high school, I had to hide my smoking from faculty members, so I would walk downtown between classes and smoke behind the storefronts of Water Street, looking out onto the murky Exeter River. During those quiet moments down on the water, sitting on gravel and dirt, surrounded by abandoned cigarette butts and beer cans and who knows what else, I felt like a rebel. I loved that feeling, that I was interesting enough to break rules, to believe rules did not apply to me.

Like most smokers, I developed elaborate practices for hiding evidence from people who might frown upon the habit – namely, my parents. I usually had an assortment of breath mints, gum, and the like on my person. If I was in a car, I would roll all the windows down as I drove, trying to convince myself that this would air me out.

It didn't take long for me to develop a pack-a-day habit, and sure, my lungs ached when I walked up stairs and sometimes I woke up coughing, and all my clothes reeked of stale smoke and the habit was becoming prohibitively expensive, but I was cool, and I was willing to make a few sacrifices to be cool in at least one small way.

CHAPTER 22

In the after, I turned to food, but there were other complicating factors. I was never athletic, even when I was slender. I was a child of the suburbs, so my parents enrolled me and my brothers in all manner of sports. Though they were both athletic, I never really excelled at any of the sports I tried, despite dutifully going to practice.

In soccer, I was a goalie. To this day, my family loves to recount the story of me sitting near the goalpost, picking dandelions in the middle of a game. I do not recall this, but it doesn't surprise me that the game held little interest for me. Flowers are pretty and soccer games are long and boring, especially when children, barely cognizant of the rules or the strategy of the game, are playing.

When I played softball, I was the catcher, but I was afraid of the ball, how it raced toward me with such force and velocity. I did everything in my power to avoid that ball, which was not at all conducive to my mastering that position. I also had no interest in running around the bases. My ideal version of the game would have had me hit the ball, have someone else run around the bases for me, and never have to play when the opposing team was at bat.

At some point, I played basketball, but I wasn't tall yet – the height would come much later, toward the end of my teens – so I had no natural advantage and was not at all adept at making baskets or defending opponents or doing anything required of someone on a basketball court. Again, I had no interest in running up and down the court. The uniforms were not flattering. My favorite position was scorekeeper. I was very good at flipping numbers over each time a new basket was scored.

In school, we played dodgeball and tetherball. We did the presidential fitness challenge and I finished the running portion last nearly every year – a mile felt like it was a marathon. In high school, sports were a significant and mandatory part of the curriculum, which was not ideal for me. I rowed crew and hated the old creaky barge of a boat we used. I played field hockey and was more interested in the merits of my field hockey stick as a weapon. Lacrosse simply made no sense to me. Ice hockey was a nightmare – spending so much time in frigid temperatures, trying to balance on two narrow blades while also basically playing soccer on ice with a small puck and awkward hockey sticks. I quickly concluded that I was allergic to sports. I still hold fast to this conclusion.

I was, however, a decent swimmer. I loved the water, the freedom of moving through it, feeling weightless. I loved being able to do things with my body in water that would never be possible on land. I even enjoyed the smell of chlorine. I once set a school record for the fifty-yard freestyle. To be clear, this was in the sixth grade, but I still feel a small rush of accomplishment at the memory because in water, using my muscles and my lungs, I was capable and strong and free.

My brothers, far more athletic, both took to soccer, my middle brother going so far as to play professionally for several years. I envied their palpable enjoyment of the sport, of athleticism, but I did not really covet that enjoyment. I've always been a woman of contradiction. My true loves were and still are books and writing stories and daydreaming. Sports were merely a distraction keeping me from what I really wanted to do.

CHAPTER 23

Throughout high school, I went through the motions, pretending to be the good student at school and the good daughter when I was talking to my parents, as my mind continued to splinter. With each passing year, I became more and more disgusted with myself. I was convinced that having been raped was my fault, that I deserved it, that what happened in the woods was all a pathetic girl like me could expect. I slept less and less because when I closed my eyes, I could feel boy bodies crushing my girl body, hurting my girl body. I smelled their sweat and beer breath and relived every terrible thing they did to me. I would wake up gasping and terrified and would spend the rest of the night staring at the ceiling or reading myself out of my body and out of my life and into something better. There was no rhyme or reason to what I read: lots of Tom Clancy and Clive Cussler for the pure escape they provided, Harlequin romances because they were so bountiful, whatever I could find in the campus library.

During the day, I went to class, which was, in

its way, another kind of escape. Academically, Exeter was intense, way more rigorous than my college classes would ever be. I loved my classes. In architecture, we had to build a vessel that would keep an egg safe if we dropped it from the roof of the building, but we could only use, like, Styrofoam and rubber bands. In an English class every Upper (or junior, to the rest of the world) had to write a Reporter at Large essay – an in-depth project for which we had to do research and interview sources and immerse ourselves in a topic that interested us. Back then I wanted to be a doctor, one of the Haitian-parent-approved professions, so I wrote about a surgeon who was my family's next-door neighbor. He was patient with my questions and allowed me to observe a surgery over spring break. While I worked on my Reporter at Large, I felt like I was so much more than a lame high school student.

I did well academically. That's how I had been raised, to be excellent, to never be satisfied with anything less. A B was a bad grade, and if I received an A-minus, I could still do better, so I did better. I did my best. I was always very high-strung about school for many reasons, not the least of which was a pressure to perform and the comfort of knowing that schoolwork, at least, was something in my control. I knew how to study and memorize and make sense of complicated things, as long as they had nothing to do with me. I also knew how much money my parents were spending on my education and so I could not fail. I could not let them down in one more way. I needed, in some small way, to feel worthy of their expectations of me.

I became more and more detached from my body, continuing to eat too much and gain weight. I only tried to lose weight when my parents made me or nagged me enough to give dieting a half-hearted try. I didn't care about getting fat. I wanted to be fat, to be big, to be ignored by men, to be safe. During the four years of high school, I probably gained 120 pounds. I racked up incredible bills using my Lion Card, the school currency system, buying so much food at The Grill, buying random crap at the school bookstore because there was a rush of solace when I ate or spent money.

As I spent all that money, I was also probably trying to keep up with the wealthy kids around me, who had their own American Express cards that they used extravagantly on weekends in Boston and exotic trips over break to Europe and to Aspen. My parents would confront me about the bills, furious at the waste of money, wanting answers for every expenditure but really wanting answers for who I had become, so different from the daughter they thought they knew. I had no answers for them. I was all self-loathing, for what had happened to me, for what I was doing to my body by gaining so much weight, for my inability to function like a normal person, for the ways I was plainly disappointing my parents.

I still nourished my commitment to being the geekiest drama geek ever to drama geek. My senior year, some friends and I wrote and produced a play on sexual violence. We all had experiences with assault that we had shared in one way or another over the years. On opening night, my parents were in the audience, and after, when I found them in the lobby, their bewilderment was palpable. They asked me how I could have come up with such a thing. It was an opportunity for me to tell them the truth of me, but I shrugged off their questions. I continued holding tight to my secret.

By the time I had to decide where to attend college, I knew I had to do whatever I could to make my parents happy, to make up for being who I was, for being a disappointment. I dutifully applied to colleges, mostly Ivy League schools and New York University. I got in everywhere except Brown University, a slight I have (clearly) never forgotten. I got my acceptance from Yale in the post office at school, surrounded by other seniors who were equally eager to find out what their futures might hold. I opened the envelope and allowed myself a flush of pride. A young white man standing near me, the kind of guy who played lacrosse, had not been accepted to the school of his choice. He looked at me with plain disgust. 'Affirmative action,' he sneered, unable to swallow the bitter truth that I, a black girl, had achieved something he could not.

If I had to go to college, and as a Haitian daughter, I *had* to go to college, I wanted to attend NYU, which had an incredible theater program. Unfortunately, my parents were adamant that it would be too distracting for me to go to college in New York City. And majoring in theater was too unrealistic, too fanciful. The final nail in the coffin of my yearning was their worry that the city was too dangerous, a concern that frustrated me, immeasurably, because I knew where danger really lurked – in the woods behind well-manicured exclusive suburban neighborhoods, at the hands of good boys from good families.

As much as I wanted to attend NYU, what I wanted even more was a break, a chance for all the noise in my head to quiet. I asked my parents if I could take a year off, because I knew I didn't have it in me to keep up appearances for much longer. I was a mess, barely holding it together, but my request was refused. Taking a year off between high school and college was not what good girls did. It never crossed my mind that I had a choice in the matter once I was told no.

I ended up choosing Yale because they had an incredible theater program and I wanted to work at the Yale Dramat like Jodie Foster had. New Haven was an hour from New York City, so I could spend the weekends in the city, I told myself. It is, of course, a bit strange to feel put upon about having to attend an Ivy League school, one of the best universities in the world, but I was a moody teenager in addition to carrying my secret, my trauma. I was in no position to face my privilege or how I took that privilege for granted.

CHAPTER 24

In the fall after I graduated from high school, my parents drove me to New Haven and moved me into my dorm on Old Campus, where all freshmen lived. I was in a fifth-floor walk-up in a quad with three other young women. I met my roommates, nice enough girls I would get along well with. My dad bought me a small blue love seat for the common room that he and another father hauled up those five flights. My mom made my bed with brand-new sheets and helped me unpack. We went out to dinner before they headed to Nebraska, where they were moving once again. It all seemed very normal. Before we parted, they wished me luck and encouraged me to work on my problem, my weight of course, and then I was on my own once more.

I have no doubt my parents were afraid to leave me at another school. The last time they did that, I gained a massive amount of weight. I'm sure they were terrified of what would happen in college, of how much bigger I could get. They didn't worry about drinking or drugs because they already knew my chosen vice. Still, they believed in the importance of education, and I think they hoped that I had some sense of self-preservation, that I would embrace the opportunity I was being given and would want to lose weight so I could be more like other girls, so I could be smaller and therefore better.

Having attended boarding school, living on campus for the first two years, I didn't have any of the typical growing pains associated with going to college. I knew how to take care of myself on a campus, or at least how to make it seem like I was taking care of myself.

But I struggled, a lot more than I had in high school. I had acquaintances but no one with whom I felt I could be honest about myself. I was unraveling so much more because there was far less supervision. There were far more temptations and ways to spend my time. New Haven, Connecticut, is a very different city from Exeter, New Hampshire, much bigger, urban, with a diverse population. There was so much more food available to me, both on and off campus – I loved going to Atticus, part bookstore, part café, with delicious salads and sandwiches. I rarely went to class, and when I was in class, little made sense. A biology teacher informed us that it was his mission to weed out the wannabes from the students who were destined to become doctors. I was weeded out, quite efficiently, because the workload was outrageously demanding. There were labs and homework and lab reports to be written according to very strict guidelines. In Calculus III, the math was so complex, so esoteric, it was almost amusing. The professor may as well have been speaking another language.

I changed my major three times in two years, from premed and biology to architecture to English. Meanwhile, I spent most of my time doing theater, as I had in high school. I never tired of being responsible for the quiet choices behind the scenes that make the theatrical spectacle work.

My days and nights were spent backstage at the Yale Dramat and in the theaters of the colleges (or dorms, anywhere else) across campus. I built sets and painted flats and ran soundboards and hung lights. One time, I accompanied a faculty adviser to a private school in Massachusetts to procure a chain-link fence that we'd use during the final scenes of *West Side Story*. I designed the set for a small college production and served as a technical director for a show in the experimental theater. I was able to forget about school, about my family, about my misery, when I worked on shows. When I was backstage or in the set shop or up on the catwalk, there were things that needed to be done and I knew how to do them. Being useful was a balm.

CHAPTER 25

That summer when I was nineteen years old marked the beginning of my lost years, and my lost years began with the Internet. When my sophomore year ended, I moved into an apartment above a small specialty grocer with an acquaintance. We weren't especially close, but at the outset, we were friendly enough to believe we could live together.

When I started college, my parents gave me a computer, a Macintosh LC II and a modem. The computer and modem were, purportedly, to help me with my studies, but really, I used them to chat with strangers all around the world on bulletin boards and in chat rooms and on IRC, an old-school chat program with thousands of channels populated by thousands of lonely people who were mostly interested in talking dirty to one another.

I spent most of my waking hours online, talking to strangers. I didn't have to be the fat, friendless loser who couldn't sleep, which is how I saw myself. I became immersed in the anonymity, and in the ability to present myself to others as I saw fit. I lost myself in feeling connected to other people for the first time in seven years. Being online offered a very particular and desperately needed thrill.

Throughout high school, I had no romantic life to speak of. I was too awkward, too shy, too much of a mess to date. I was invisible to the boys at my high school because of my blackness, because of my size, because of my complete indifference toward my appearance. Because I read so much, I was a romantic in my heart of hearts, but my desire to be part of a romantic story was a very intellectual, detached one. I liked the idea of a boy asking me out, taking me on a date, kissing me, but I did not want to actually be alone with a boy, because a boy could hurt me.

The men I talked to online allowed me to enjoy the idea of romance and love and lust and sex while keeping my body safe. I could pretend to be thin and sexy and confident.

I discovered forums for rape and sexual abuse survivors, where, as with when I read *The Courage to Heal,* I saw that I was not alone. In those online forums, I saw that horrible things happened to so many girls and sometimes boys. I saw that however bad my secret was, many people had far worse secrets.

In IRC chat rooms, I talked to people in the BDSM community, and I learned about safe, sane, and consensual sexual encounters, where power was exchanged, but you could have a safe word to make things stop when you wanted them to stop. I learned that there were people who would take the right kind of no as no, and that was powerful, intoxicating. I wanted to know so much more about safe ways to say no.

I had a more expansive vocabulary, now, for what happened in the woods. At twelve years old, I had no such words. I just knew that these boys had forced me to have sex with them, had used my body in ways I did not know a girl body could be used. Thanks to books and therapy and my new friends online, I knew ever more clearly that there was a thing called rape. I knew that when a woman said no, men were supposed to listen and stop what they were doing. I knew that it wasn't my fault that I had been raped. There was a quiet thrill to having this new vocabulary, but in many ways, I did not feel like that vocabulary could apply to me. I was too damaged, too weak to deserve absolution. It was not as easy to believe these truths as it was to know them.

CHAPTER 26

A couple weeks before my junior year was supposed to begin, I disappeared. I told no one where I was going, not my roommate, who was increasingly and justifiably fed up with my erratic behavior, or my acquaintances, or even my parents. I flew to San Francisco because I had met a man in his forties on an online bulletin board and we had mutual . . . interests. For the first time in my life, I felt wanted, and though I felt no real desire for this man, being wanted was enough. I put my body in danger even though I knew better, but I wanted nothing more than to leave my life as I knew it. I grabbed at my only way out.

For all the trouble I've known, I have also been very lucky. This older man was strange but kind. He never hurt me. He never forced me to do anything I did not want to do. He looked out for me and introduced me to other strange but kind people who accepted me as I was – young, lost, and a complete fucking wreck – without taking advantage of me. We went to San Francisco to attend some parties, where I met many of the people I had been chatting with online for months. After a raucous time, he invited me to follow him to Scottsdale, Arizona, a suburb of Phoenix, where he lived. I didn't want to return to my life. I couldn't. So I didn't.

I had no money, only a few days' worth of clothing. No one who loved me knew where I was. I was thrilled. I felt free because I didn't have to pretend to be the good Ivy League girl anymore for my parents or anyone else.

I spent nearly a year in Phoenix. I lost my mind and I didn't even try to pull the pieces of myself back together. I just did whatever I wanted. I did the kinds of things that the good girl I had long pretended to be would never dream of doing. There was no more pretending I was a straight-A student or a girl who cared about grades or a good daughter or a good anything. Completely unmoored from my previous life, I could be a blank slate. I could reinvent myself. I could take the kinds of risks that would have, not long before, been unthinkable. I could complete the break that had long been growing between me and my family and everything I had ever known.

I worked the graveyard shift at a phone sex company in downtown Phoenix with a bunch of other lost girls. I mostly sat in my booth and did crossword puzzles while I talked to lonely men who wanted nothing more than the fantasy of a woman who might listen to them for ten minutes or an hour or two. Around four in the morning, on our lunch break, we would get food, greasy terrible food, from a Jack in the Box across the street. I was fat and I continued to eat to get fatter and I talked to men without having to be touched by men. When my shift was over, I went home and sometimes invited my coworkers over, and we sat around the pool at this man's house, sleeping with our sunglasses on as the Arizona sun burned into our skin.

One day the man who brought me to Arizona taught me to shoot a gun with wax bullets. It was exhilarating, holding a gun in my hand, the power of pulling the trigger, even if the bullets only hit an inanimate target with a quiet splat. I thought about turning the gun on the boys who had hurt me. I thought about turning the gun on myself.

Most of the choices I made during my lost year were ill advised. I was reckless. I did not care about my body because my body was nothing. I let men, mostly, do terrible things to my body. I let them hurt me because I had already been hurt and so, really, I was looking for someone to finish what had already been started.

Bottomless. Fearless. This is the reputation I developed in my social circle. One of those things was true.

I went home with strangers. One man invited me over while his wife slept on the floor next to the bed where we lay. His floor was covered in cat litter. I can still remember the crunch of it beneath my bare feet as I snuck out the next morning, walked to a pay phone, and called the man I lived with to come get me. I started dating women because I naïvely thought that with women, I might be safe. I thought women would be easier to understand.

For a couple of months, I lived with the man, and later, I got an apartment with a couple who would end up taking my share of the rent money and never paying the rent. When we were evicted, rather abruptly, a few months after I'd moved in, I was the only one who was shocked.

My parents eventually found me with the help, I assume, of a private investigator. I have never asked. They had my brother Michael Jr call me, somehow knowing I would not hang up on him, the baby of the family. We reconnected, tentatively. I learned that my father had gone to New Haven and packed up my apartment, made what amends he could with the roommate I had left in the lurch so irresponsibly. Once we reconnected, my dad shipped me some of my stuff. He paid my outstanding bills. He fathered me despite everything I was doing to be unparented.

And then it all ended. I came home to an eviction notice on my apartment door. The couple I was living with was frantically packing all their belongings as if everything were just fine. I panicked because I had, in my still relatively sheltered and privileged life, never known such a thing. As I cried and freaked out, I packed my stuff into a trunk and left it with a friend. I considered my options but didn't want to go home. I wasn't ready. With what money I had, I bought a plane ticket to Minneapolis. I went to Minnesota, in the dead of winter, to stay with a girl I met on the Internet. This would become a pattern – meeting lovers online. At first, I did it because it felt safer and I could be sexual without having to actually be sexual. Then, as I got fatter, it was a way to meet people and hopefully charm them with personality before having to show them the truth of my big body. I thought the girl in Minnesota was the love of my life. This would also become a pattern. Two weeks later, I realized she wasn't the love of my life. She was a stranger and I had nothing, no money, nowhere to live, no job. I broke down and called my parents. My father told me to go to the Minneapolis airport and I did and there was a plane ticket waiting for me. Again, he fathered me.

Though they did not have to, though they were frantic with worry, my parents welcomed me home. They had questions and anger and hurt and I couldn't do much about any of that. I could not tell them the truth. I could not explain why I continued to gain so much weight. I could not figure out how to be less of a disappointment. And still, I knew I had a home to return to, a home where I would be welcomed and loved.

I was still a mess. I spent a lot of time in my room, on my computer, tying up the phone line with my modem, which did not go over well with the rest of my family. It was easier to lose myself in the virtual world than to try and put my life back together or face these people who thought they knew me. I was still broken and I liked how it felt to simply accept that everything was wrong and couldn't be set right. It felt good to not try and pretend.

CHAPTER 27

After several tense months of living at home in Omaha, I moved to Lincoln, about fifty miles away. I wanted my independence and my 'space' and to feel like an adult even though I was so far from being an adult. I was twenty years old and I felt like I was twelve years old and I felt like I was twenty years old and I felt like I was a hundred years old. I knew nothing but thought I knew everything.

The apartment, subsidized by my parents of course, was a one-bedroom with a tiny kitchen and a balcony, where I smoked with continued enthusiasm.

I went to my parents' house often, and I would stock up on toilet paper and groceries from my mother's pantry. Things were still fractured between us, but I knew, as always, that I had a home. I had a very well-financed crack-up. I did not go hungry even as I hungered for so much.

To at least try to support myself, I held a series of odd jobs – adult video store clerk, telemarketer, Gallup poll taker, loan consolidator at a student loan company – and quickly realized that without a college degree I was only ever going to work odd jobs for minimum wage. I was readmitted to Yale, but the thought of returning to New Haven was unbearable. I turned twenty-one and celebrated by buying a six-pack of Corona even though I hate the taste and stink of beer. Later that night, a woman I was casually dating called, and when I mentioned it was my birthday and I was sitting alone in my apartment, with a sweaty six-pack of cheap beer, she offered to show me a good time. I don't even remember what we did. I had no friends. I ended up finishing my degree through a brief residency program at Vermont College, which was, at the time, part of Norwich University – a military college in Vermont. I wrote and wrote and wrote.

I very much wanted to be a writer, so I enrolled in the MA program in creative writing at the University of Nebraska–Lincoln. I worked at night and went to school during the day. I was broke all the time, which is not to be confused with being poor. I had a safety net and I knew I had a safety net, and though there were many days I was fueled by ramen, still I did not go hungry while I hungered. I rarely slept because it was in sleep that I was forced to confront myself, my past. I was tormented by terrible dreams, memories really, of those boys, the woods, my body at their lack of mercy.

At the university, I went to classes and learned about Victorian literature and cultural theory and postcolonialism and I sat in workshops with students who were surprisingly generous in their feedback about my writing, given common wisdom about writing workshops. I served as an editorial assistant for *Prairie Schooner*, the program's literary magazine, and was mostly relegated to opening all the incoming mail – hundreds of submissions a week from writers like me who just wanted to be discovered. It was there that I learned that one of the best ways to measure where you stand as a writer is to work at a literary magazine. We received all manner of submissions. People sent in diaries, odes to their cats, entire novels or books of poetry, all carefully printed out and stuffed into manila envelopes. There were many submissions from prisoners who were just as lonely as I was, who had found their voices in their prison cells and wanted their voices to be heard. I pored over the cover letters from all these writers who would share seemingly anything about their lives.

When I got home at night, I generally went straight to my computer, where I wrote story after story, mostly about women and their hurt because it was the only way I could think of to bleed out all the hurt I was feeling. I frequented newsgroups and chat rooms for survivors of sexual assault. Though I couldn't tell anyone in my real life what had happened, I unburdened myself to strangers on the Internet. I blogged, mostly about the minutiae of my life, hoping, I think, to be seen and heard. I loved and craved the freedom of being online and being free from my life and my body. I ate and ate and ate but rarely was any of the food I ate memorable for any reason but the quantity. I ate mindlessly, just to fill the gaping wound of me or to *try* to fill the gaping wound of me. No matter how much I ate, I still hurt and I was still terrified of other people and the memories I couldn't escape. I managed to put together a collection of short stories for my thesis, entitled *How Small the World*, and successfully defended my thesis and then I was done with school and I had no idea what to do so I got a job working at the university as a writer for the College of Engineering. I tried to do what was expected of me. Some days, I tried really hard.

CHAPTER 28

As I spent more time working at the College of Engineering, I realized that when I had dreamed of making a living as a writer, I probably should have been more specific about what, exactly, I meant by that. And still, every day I got to write. I had my own office and a computer on which I could play solitaire and work on my own writing. I mostly wrote articles about faculty research – things that I knew nothing about and that the faculty were more than eager to explain to me – on robotic construction equipment, aerogels that could be used in space, defenses against bioterrorism, innovative uses for RFID chips.

The job was fine, by far the best job I had ever had, making the most money I had ever made even though I was not making much money at all. I had a great, encouraging supervisor named Constance, who made me a much better writer. I learned how to use the Adobe Creative Suite. I worked with undergraduate engineering students as the adviser of their magazine.

And still, I would sit in professors' offices listening to them talk about their research and think, *I could totally do what they do.* Certainly, that was a bit grandiose, but I was working ten-hour days, always at someone else's whim. I envied the freedom faculty seemed to have, teaching two or three times a week, setting their own schedules and being handsomely compensated. I wanted to live that life. Throughout my MA program, I had always intended to get my PhD, but I was going to get my PhD in creative writing and write my great Haitian American novel and get a teaching job and be set for life.

And then, as one of my work duties, I went to the annual conference for the National Society of Black Engineers to man a recruitment table for the College of Engineering. The woman whose table was across the aisle from mine throughout the conference, Betty, began talking to me about the school she worked for, Michigan Technological University, and how they had a great technical communication program. I had never heard of Michigan Tech, and was certain that I'd be staying at UNL. After the conference, though, she stayed in touch and she was persistent. Then the woman I thought I was in a relationship with broke up with me, on Valentine's Day, via e-mail, and suddenly, I wanted to be as far away from Lincoln as possible. I applied to Michigan Tech, was accepted, and they made me an offer I could not refuse – enough money to nearly match my salary, teaching opportunities, tuition remission, and terrible health insurance. That summer, I moved to Hancock, Michigan, sight unseen, to attend a doctoral program at a school I had never heard of in a field I knew nothing about. My brother Michael Jr transferred to Michigan Tech and joined me. As we drove into town, we both realized that we had no idea what we were getting ourselves into. The Upper Peninsula was so very remote. The two-lane country highways we took for hours were dwarfed by trees thick with leaves. There were deer everywhere as the sun set, so we slowed to a crawl. When I met my landlord, who lived in the upstairs unit of an old building where she and her deceased husband had run a dry cleaner, she stood behind her latched screen door as my brother and I stood on the porch. She peered out at me and said, 'You didn't sound like a colored girl on the phone.' I was thirty years old.

CHAPTER 29

There was something comforting about graduate school and living a life of the mind. My body didn't matter because I was in school, taking classes and learning things. I was learning how to teach on the job. I had very specific responsibilities that demanded nearly all of my focus, my time and energy.

But I couldn't forget my body. I could not escape it. I didn't know how, and the world was always there to remind me.

On my first day of teaching, a Monday, I threw up before class because I was terrified, though not of the teaching itself. I would be teaching freshman composition, and while managing a classroom is always a challenge, I felt comfortable imparting onto my students the basics of writing persuasively. What I feared was my appearance and what they would think of me. I worried that if they didn't like me, they would make fun of me, mocking my weight, and I was not at all sure how to make them like me when I felt so very unlikable, and always had. I worried about stamina and whether I would be able to stand for fifty minutes. I worried about sweating in front of them and how they would judge me for it. I worried about what to wear, because my standard uniform of jeans and T-shirts was too casual and what little dressy clothing I did have would have been way too dressy for the classroom.

The good thing about school is that students have been trained, from an early age, to follow the rules. They come to class and generally sit and behave in an orderly fashion. When you tell them to do things, they do those things. I walked into my first classroom, my heart pounding, sweating everywhere, my head ringing with all of my fears and insecurities. I was carrying a big box of Legos because I figured, if nothing else, the students might enjoy playing with toys. At first, they didn't seem to realize I was their teacher, and I was not sure if they were unsure because of my size, my race, or what I vainly hoped was my youthful appearance. When I stood at the front of the class-room, they hushed, and realized I was the teacher. I took attendance, my legs rubbery with anxiety, and then went into discussing the syllabus, the nature of the class and what would be expected of them – regular attendance, active participation, homework turned in on time, no plagiarism and the like. It was reassuring to have these adminis-trative details to go over with the students, but when I was done discussing the syllabus, I actually had to teach and my anxiety rushed right back through me.

At the end of that first class, as the students filed out of the room, I wanted to collapse with relief because I had survived those fifty minutes of being fat in front of twenty-two eighteen- and nineteen-year-olds. And then I realized I was going to have to do it all over again, on Wednesday and Friday, week in and week out for the entire semester.

I went to my classes. I taught. I studied. I tried to make friends and did, with a small measure of success. On weekends, I played poker at a casino in Baraga, the Ojibwe reservation about forty miles away, hunched around the table with strange men, where I was intent on taking their money, which often I did. I still didn't sleep much. I kept eating, trying to find some kind of peace.

And then, one day, I was walking home from the gas station across the street, where I had gone to buy cigarettes. I wore a knit cap on my head, a ratty T-shirt, and pajama pants. I looked terrible, but no one at the Citgo cared. I didn't care, either. A man started calling after me, shouting, 'Hey, Casino Girl,' which only made me want to run. I assumed that he was going to make fun of me because I had long become accustomed to people, men mostly, calling out cruelties from their cars, their bicycles, when they walked on by – letting me know exactly what they thought of my body.

This was not that. He followed me to my apartment and up the stairs, so I quickly closed the screen door, latched it, and stared out at him. 'You play poker at the casino,' he said, and I nodded, reluctantly. I tried to place him but couldn't. He looked like every other white guy I saw around town – dark, shaggy hair, a beard, wearing flannel and denim and work boots. 'You're always talking shit at the poker table. Do you wanna come hang out with me and my friends?' He pointed toward the distance. 'Absolutely not,' I told him, wanting him to go away, but he was mighty persistent. I was unsure what he wanted from me, but I knew it couldn't be anything good. Maybe he wanted me to go meet his friends so they could hurt me. Maybe he wanted money. I ran through the possibilities as he kept yammering on. Finally he said he needed to get back to his friends, and I closed my door, unsettled. I couldn't sleep that night, staring at the ceiling, worrying about the strange man who followed me home.

He kept coming back, night after night, and would always knock, then stand on my porch when I finally came to the door, talking to me through the screen, never trying to come inside. Eventually it dawned on me that he was trying to ask me out. We went out to dinner at the nearby Ramada, which had a lousy restaurant but a good bar. His name was Jon. He was a logger. He loved to hunt and fish. He loved Lakers basketball. He had never lived anywhere but Michigan's Upper Peninsula.

I was always skeptical of his attention, always waiting for him to reveal his true, cruel self, but day after day and week after week, he was good to me. He was solid. He ignored my casual barbs and resisted any and all attempts to push him away. He drank too much, but he was a happy drunk, the kind to laugh at his own jokes and fall asleep with a smile on his face. I quit smoking because I was getting older and realized I had been smoking for eighteen years and that I had to at least try to love myself enough to give up one of my terrible but beloved habits.

I was online all the time, starting to blog for websites like *HTMLGiant* and *The Rumpus*. I discovered social networking. I started sending my writing out into the world again. Jon called anyone I knew online one of my 'little friends in the computer.' Some weekends, he would take me to his camp, the Upper Peninsula version of a remote lake cabin. There was no Internet up there and barely any cell phone service. I had to disconnect from the safety of the virtual world and be present in the real world, with him. He was the first man who touched me with any kind of gentleness, even when I asked him not to. He loved me and, over time, I realized I loved him too. We had a good relationship, one with more ups than downs.

And then I came to the end of my doctoral program. I got a job teaching at Eastern Illinois University. I was starting to make a name for myself as a writer. I had every reason to feel hopeful. Jon and I had countless conversations about what we would do. He wanted me to stay. A part of me wanted to do it, to just settle down and become a logger's wife. But a bigger part of me wanted him

112

to follow me because I had worked so hard for five years. I had accomplished something not many people, and even fewer black women, accomplish. I wanted to believe in our love story. I waited for him to make the grand gesture I wanted and needed from him. I wanted to believe I was worthy of that grand gesture.

Jon and I had no dramatic arguments as we faced the end of my time in the UP. After I graduated, he helped me move to Illinois. We went to IKEA and shopped for furniture. He assembled book-shelves and a coffee table and checked the locks on the doors in my new apartment. We said good-bye in a hundred different ways without actually saying 'Good-bye.' Jon's eyes were red when he headed back home. So were mine. We stayed in touch, and for a time, there was a genuine yearning between us for the idea of what we could be. And still, that grand gesture never came. I fell back into the familiar embrace of self-loathing. I blamed myself. I blamed my body.

PART III

CHAPTER 30

I often refer to my twenties as the worst years of my life because that's exactly what they were. From one year to the next, though, things got better in that I became more functional as an adult. I was able to accumulate degrees and get better jobs. Slowly but surely, I tried to repair my relationship with my parents and redeem myself in their eyes. In the before I had been a good girl, so I knew how to play that role. Some part of me was still willing to play that role after my lost year in Arizona so that, despite my desperate loneliness, I might still be connected to something – work, writing, family.

But.

During my twenties, my personal life was an unending disaster. I did not meet many people who treated me with any kind of kindness or respect. I was a lightning rod for indifference, disdain, and outright aggression, and I tolerated all of this because I knew I didn't deserve any better, not after how I had been ruined and not after how I continued to ruin my body.

My friendships, and I use that term loosely,

were fleeting and fragile and often painful, with people who generally wanted something from me and were gone as soon as they got that something. I was so lonely I was willing to tolerate these relationships. The faint resemblance of human connection was enough. It had to be enough even though it wasn't.

Food was the only place of solace. Alone, in my apartment, I could soothe myself with food. Food didn't judge me or demand anything from me. When I ate, I did not have to be anything but myself. And so I gained a hundred pounds and then another hundred and then another hundred.

In some ways, it feels like the weight just appeared on my body one day. I was a size 8 and then I was a size 16 and then I was a size 28 and then I was a size 42.

In other ways, I was intimately aware of every single pound that accumulated and clung to my body. And everyone around me was also intimately aware. My family's concern became a constant chorus of nagging, always well intended, but mostly a reminder of how I was a failure in the most basic of my human responsibilities – maintaining my body. They were relentless in asking me what I was going to do about my 'problem.' They offered advice. They tried tough love. They offered to send me to specialists and spas. They offered financial incentives and new wardrobes and new cars. There is nothing they would not have done to help me solve the problem of my body.

They mean well, my parents. They love me. They understand the world as it is, and how there is no room for people of my size. They know that the older I get, the harder it will become to live at this size. They worry about my health and my happiness. They are good parents. My parents also want to understand – they are intellectual, smart, practical. They want my weight to be a problem they can address with the intellect they apply to other problems. They want to understand how I could have let this happen, let my body become so big, so out of control. We have that in common.

And still. They are my personal Obesity Crisis Intervention team. They have been actively pursuing the problem of my body since I was fourteen years old. I love them so I accept this, sometimes with grace and sometimes without. It is only now, in my early forties, that I have started to put my foot down and say, when they try to broach the conversation of my body, 'No. I will not discuss my body with you. No. My body, how I move it, how I nourish it, is not your business.'

There was a time when every conversation included some kind of question about my weight. My parents, and my father in particular, make inquiries as to whether I am dieting, exercising, and/or losing weight as if all I am is my big fat body. But they love me. This is what I remind myself so I can forgive them.

My father is the more passionate one in this crusade. Over the years, he has gifted me weight-loss programs and books on weight loss, particularly those endorsed by Oprah. One year, it was Richard Simmons's *Deal-a-Meal*. He has sent me brochures. He has told me to take time off from school because 'all those degrees you're getting aren't going to do you any good, because no one is going to hire you at your size.' He has told me, 'I am only telling you what no one else will,' but of course, he is telling me what the world is always telling me, everywhere I go. When he hears of a new weight-loss drug or program on the radio, on TV, at the airport, anywhere, he is quick to call me and ask me if I have heard of what he hopes is the silver bullet solution to the problem of my body. He has so much hope for what I could be if only I could overcome my body. His hope breaks my heart.

My mother is subtler and she frames her worry primarily around my health. She often discusses the health risks of obesity with me – diabetes, heart attack, stroke. She worries that my caretaking will fall to her if I do succumb to a terrible illness, and that she won't be up to the task.

My brothers care too, and I know they also worry, but they are my brothers so they don't pressure me about weight loss. They are my defenders and also my tormentors. They have a song, the 'humongous' song. My middle brother loves to serenade me with it. 'When I say humongous, humong la laaaaa,' he will screech, and then everyone will laugh because it is oh so funny. It wasn't funny when I was a teenager and it isn't funny now, but the song persists. I often become irate when they sing this song. My body is not a joke or fodder for amusement, but, I suppose, to many people, it is.

My family's constant pressure to lose weight made me stubborn, even though the only person I was really hurting was myself. The constant pressure made me refuse to lose weight to punish these people who claimed to love me but wouldn't accept me as I was. It became easier to drown out that chorus of concern, to tolerate the horrible ways people treated me, to ignore that I could no longer buy clothes in the mall, or at Lane Bryant, and sometimes not even at Catherines. I became resentful that the only thing anyone ever wanted to focus on was my body, always unruly and disappointing. I shut down completely. I went through the motions. I learned how to tune out my parents, my brothers, people on the street. I learned how to live in my head, where I could ignore the world that refused to accept me, where I could block out the memories of the boys I couldn't forget, no matter how much time and distance yawned between me and them.

For years at a time, there was me, and the woman I saw myself as while living in my head, and the woman who had to carry around my overweight body. They were not the same person. They couldn't be, or I wouldn't have survived any of it.

CHAPTER 31

When you're overweight, your body becomes a matter of public record in many respects. Your body is constantly and prominently on display. People project assumed narratives onto your body and are not at all interested in the truth of your body, whatever that truth might be.

Fat, much like skin color, is something you cannot hide, no matter how dark the clothing you wear, or how diligently you avoid horizontal stripes. You may become very adept at playing the role of wallflower. You may learn how to be the life of the party so that people are too busy laughing at or with you to focus on the elephant in the room. You may do whatever you have to do to survive a world that has little patience or compassion for a body like yours.

Regardless of what you do, your body is the subject of public discourse with family, friends, and strangers alike. Your body is subject to commentary when you gain weight, lose weight, or maintain your unacceptable weight. People are quick to offer you statistics and information about the dangers of obesity, as if you are not only fat but also incredibly stupid, unaware, delusional about the realities of your body and a world that is vigorously inhospitable to that body. This commentary is often couched as *concern*, as people only having your *best interests* at heart. They forget that you are a person. You are your body, nothing more, and your body should damn well become less.

CHAPTER 32

An epidemic is the spread of a contagion. It is the unstoppable march of an infectious disease across humanity. Throughout history, there have been many epidemics – measles, influenza, smallpox, the bubonic plague, yellow fever, malaria, cholera – but none is so deadly and pervasive, according to countless news reports, as the obesity epidemic. Instead of fever, leaking pustules, swollen glands, or lesions, your symptoms are girth and sheer mass. The obese body is the expression of excess, decadence, and weakness. The obese body is a site of massive infection. It is a losing battleground in a war between willpower and food and metabolism in which you are the ultimate loser.

Rarely does a day go by, particularly in the United States, without some new article discussing the obesity epidemic, the crisis. These articles are often harsh, alarmist, and filled with false concern for people afflicted by this epidemic and a profoundly genuine concern for life as we know it. Oh, the burdens on the health-care system, these articles lament. Obesity, these articles ultimately say, is killing us all and costing us an unacceptable fortune.

There is, certainly, a very small grain of truth in these articles, in this frenzied panic. And also, there is fear, because no one wants to be infected by obesity, largely because people know how they see and treat and think about fat people and don't want such a fate to befall them.

CHAPTER 33

As a fat woman, I often see my existence reduced to statistics, as if with cold, hard numbers, our culture might make sense of what hunger can become. According to government statistics, the obesity epidemic costs between $147 and $210 billion a year, though there is little clear information as to how researchers arrive at that overwhelming number. What exactly are the costs associated with obesity? The methodology is irrelevant. What matters is that fat is expensive and therefore a grave problem. Fat people are a drain on resources, what with needing health care and medication for their all too human bodies. Many people act like fat people are reaching directly into their wallets, the fat of other people a burden on their personal bottom line.

Statistics also reveal that 34.9 percent of Americans are obese and 68.6 percent of Americans are obese or overweight. The definitions of 'overweight' and 'obese' are often vague and obscured by arbitrary measures like BMI or various other indexes. And this just in: the obesity epidemic has recently crossed the Atlantic Ocean, and now many Europeans are falling prey to what is quickly becoming a pandemic – an epidemic of global proportions. What matters most is that too many people are fat. The epidemic must be stopped, by any means necessary.

CHAPTER 34

F ew areas of popular culture focus on obesity more than reality television, and that focus is glaring, harsh, often cruel.

The Biggest Loser is an unholy union of capitalism and the weight-loss industrial complex. On the surface, *The Biggest Loser* is a television show about weight loss, but really, it's anti-obesity propaganda, offering wish fulfillment for people with unruly, overweight bodies, both on the show and in the viewing audience. The show allows the home viewer to feel motivated without actually doing anything. If the viewer does get motivated, they can participate at home and feel like they are, in some small way, part of the show. Meanwhile, they also have the satisfaction of watching fat people become less fat from one week to the next while competing for $250,000.

I watched the first few seasons of *The Biggest Loser* avidly. The show offered the ultimate fat-girl fantasy – you go to a 'ranch' for a few months, and under the pressure of intense personal trainers, dangerously low caloric intake, the manipulations of reality show producers, and the constant surveillance of television cameras, you lose the weight you've never been able to lose on your own.

During those first few seasons, I often toyed with the idea of auditioning to appear on the show, though, realistically, that could never happen. I'm too shy. I would go through withdrawal from the Internet. I can't work out without music. If Jillian Michaels screamed at me, I would shut down or cry like a baby or strangle her. At the time, I was a vegetarian and I was concerned because I don't eat Jennie-O turkey, a product the show shamelessly hawked for years by way of product placement. Appearing on the show simply was not and is not feasible for me.

The longer *The Biggest Loser* has been on the air, however, the more the show has disturbed me. There is the constant shaming of fat people and the medical professionals who take every opportunity to crow about how near death these obese contestants are. There are the trainers, with their undeniably, implausibly perfect bodies, demanding perfection from people who have, for whatever reason, not had a previously healthy relationship with their bodies. There is the spectacle of the contestants pushing themselves in inhuman ways – crying and sweating and vomiting – visibly purging their bodies of weakness. This is not a show about people becoming empowered through fitness, though the show's slick marketing would have you believe that.

The Biggest Loser is a show about fat as an enemy

that must be destroyed, a contagion that must be eradicated. This is a show about unruly bodies that must be disciplined by any means necessary, so that through that discipline, the obese might become more acceptable members of society. They might find happiness, which can, according to the show, according to cultural norms, only be found through thinness. When we watch shows like *The Biggest Loser* and its many imitators, we are practically begging some power beyond ourselves, 'Take these all too human bodies, and make what you will of them.'

With the dramatic reveal of Rachel Frederickson, the Season 15 winner of *The Biggest Loser*, those of us who watch finally had an unimpeachable reason to be visibly outraged about the show and its practices, even though the show has been on the air and offering a damaging narrative about weight loss since 2004.

When her season began, Frederickson weighed 260 pounds. At her final weigh-in, on live television, she weighed 105, a 60 percent loss in mere months. During this reveal, even trainers Bob Harper and Jillian Michaels gaped at Frederickson's gaunt body. She had disciplined her body the way she'd been asked to, but apparently, she had disciplined her body a bit too much. The biggest loser, we now know, should lose, but only so much. There are so many rules for the body – often unspoken and ever-shifting.

In an interview, Harper would later say, 'I was

stunned. That would be the word. I mean, we've never had a contestant come in at 105 pounds.' There was a wide range of responses in the press and on social media in the wake of seeing Rachel Frederickson's new body. Her body, like most women's bodies, instantly became a public text, a site of discourse, only now because she had taken her weight loss too far. She had disciplined her body too much.

As of late, several former contestants have leveled many accusations against the show, alleging that producers used forced dehydration, severely restricted caloric intake, and encouraged the use of weight-loss drugs and more to help contestants reach their goals, to make for better television. Even more damning was a medical study of one season's participants, led by metabolism expert Kevin Hall. The study found that thirteen of the fourteen contestants' metabolisms continued slowing even after their significant weight loss. This slowed metabolism contributed to the contestants gaining back most, if not all or more, of the weight they had lost on the show. The results are a stark reminder that weight loss is a challenge that the medical establishment has not yet overcome. It is certainly not a challenge a reality television show has overcome. It's no wonder that so many of us struggle with our bodies.

In the two months after her big reveal, Frederickson gained twenty pounds and reached, apparently, a more acceptable but still appropriately disciplined size. She explained that she lost so much weight because she was trying to win the $250,000 prize, but those of us who deny ourselves and try so hard to discipline our bodies know better. Rachel Frederickson was doing exactly what we asked of her, and what too many of us would, if we could, ask of ourselves.

CHAPTER 35

There are any number of weight-loss shows in the vein of *The Biggest Loser*. On *Extreme Makeover: Weight Loss*, the show takes a slightly more realistic approach to the project of significant weight loss, following fat people on their 'weight-loss journey' over a year. The trainer is far more genial than those on *The Biggest Loser*. We see more of the genuine struggle of weight loss, how it's not something that can be neatly accomplished and packaged for a televised audience. The message, though, is the same – that self-worth and happiness are inextricably linked to thinness.

Some shows are hell-bent on exploitation. On *Fit to Fat to Fit*, physically impeccable trainers gain weight so they can better empathize with their clients. Then they have to lose the weight again so as to return to their natural, more perfect forms. The show chronicles their initial joy of eating with abandon, followed by the apparent misery of having to eat fast food and being fat, and finally the lasting satisfaction of these trainers returning to their preferred state of impeccable fitness. Their clients are, by and large, accessories to the tragic, then triumphant gain-loss narrative the show loves.

Khloé Kardashian, who has often been tormented by tabloids for weighing a bit more than 110 pounds, is hosting a show for E! called *Revenge Body*, where participants get revenge on someone who has wronged them by losing weight and getting into shape. It's a hell of a thing, this idea that the way to truly settle old scores is to get thinner and fitter. The very premise of the show suggests that if you're fat, the people who have wronged you are probably gloating and reveling in your circumstance.

On *My 600-lb Life*, the show's morbidly obese subjects travel to Houston, where one Dr Younan Nowzaradan – or Dr Now, as he is often called – performs weight-loss surgery on them. On this show, fat is treated as a pitiable spectacle. *My 600-lb Life* revels in the stories of people who are so overwhelmed by their unruly bodies that they often have to be helped out of their homes by EMTs. They are at the point of no return, their bodies failing them, their loved ones exasperated and ready to walk away. The fat people on this show eat outrageous quantities of food and are often suffering from unresolved trauma. They also suffer from any number of physical ailments. They are, in many ways, cautionary tales. Watch her, out of breath, making her way to the mailbox. Watch him, sunken into the couch, eating from a greasy bag of hamburgers. Watch her struggle to get in and out of her car, the steering wheel choking her gut. We see these people at their most vulnerable, in ill-fitting, often oversized clothes, if they can even wear clothes, their corpulence spreading everywhere, defying convention, defying our cultural norms.

Each episode has a very familiar narrative arc, in which we meet the subject and learn about their life, the seemingly miserable limitations of it. Then they meet Dr Now, who chastises them and their loved ones for letting things get so out of hand. He tends to be palpably distressed by his patient and their family. Dr Now often requires that these people go on a 1,200-calorie-a-day diet so they can lose fifty pounds before he will perform the weight-loss surgery. He does the surgery and it always goes well and then the subject sees a therapist and stumbles along trying to live and eat differently. This show loves to gratuitously display the fat body, all the excess, the mounds of flesh. The surgeries are graphic, and we see insides, globules of fat being shoved aside by medical instruments, as the obese body is medically brought to heel. Through medical intervention, the show offers redemption or, at least, a chance at redemption. Each episode tries to end on a hopeful note, but sometimes, even with medical intervention, there is no happy ending, which for the show is a drastically thinner body. In that, *My 600-lb Life* offers some truth.

I hate these shows, but clearly I watch them. I

watch them even though sometimes they enrage me and sometimes they break my heart and all too often they reveal painfully familiar experiences of loneliness, depression, and genuine suffering born of living in a world that cannot accommodate overweight bodies. I watch these shows because even though I know how damaging and unrealistic they are, some part of me still yearns for the salvation they promise.

CHAPTER 36

It's not just reality TV that is obsessed with weight. If you watch enough daytime television, particularly on 'women's networks,' you are treated to an endless parade of commercials about weight-loss products and diet foods – means of disciplining the body that will also fatten the coffers of one corporation or another. These commercials drive me crazy. They encourage self-loathing. They tell us, most of us, that we aren't good enough in our bodies as they are. They offer us the cruelest aspiration. In these commercials, women swoon at the possibility of satisfying their hunger with somewhat repulsive foods while also maintaining an appropriately slim figure. The joy women express over fat-free yogurt and 100-calorie snack packs is not to be believed. Every time I watch a yogurt commercial I think, *My god, I want to be that happy. I really do.*

It is a powerful lie to equate thinness with self-worth. Clearly, this lie is damn convincing because the weight-loss industry thrives. Women continue to try to bend themselves to societal will. Women continue to hunger. And so do I.

In one of her many commercials for Weight Watchers, Jessica Simpson smiles brightly and says, 'I started losing weight right away. I started smiling right away.' In her commercials for Weight Watchers, Jennifer Hudson shrieks about her newfound happiness and how, through weight loss – not, say, winning an Oscar – she achieved success. These are just two of many weight-loss advertisements that equate happiness with thinness and, by the law of inverses, obesity with misery.

Valerie Bertinelli was a Jenny Craig spokeswoman who proudly showed off her 'new body' in 2012. Though she lost forty pounds, she then gained some of that weight back. For that crime, her penance was to go on the talk show circuit, trying to fight fat shaming. She would, of course, eventually head back to the gym when her press tour was over. She wanted, according to ABC News, to be 'back in bikini shape by summer.' Kirstie Alley also rejoined the Jenny Craig fold around that time. 'Without a coach helping us along the way, I don't think someone can make it for the long haul,' Alley said. The public weight-struggle spectacle is a popular fallback for once-famous women who yearn to recapture their former glory.

Women, for that is whom these ecstatic diet food commercials and celebrity weight-loss endorsements are for, *can* have it all when they eat the right foods and follow the right diets and pay the right price.

What does it say about our culture that the desire for weight loss is considered a default feature of womanhood?

CHAPTER 37

For most of my life, Oprah Winfrey has been a cultural icon who publicly struggles with her weight. For most of my life I have also struggled with my weight, though, mercifully, out of the public eye. Oprah has lost weight and celebrated that victory. She has gained weight and lamented that failure. In 1988, when her talk show was at the height of its popularity, she lost nearly seventy pounds on a liquid diet. She dragged a bright red Radio Flyer wagon filled with animal fat onto the stage of her show. She was resplendent, hair teased high, black turtleneck, tight jeans, as she performed her disgust at the spectacle of such fat, straining to try and lift the bag from the wagon. She was performing penance for the sin of having been fat.

This is the woman who brought us the idea of living our best life, of becoming our most authentic selves. And yet. In 2015, Winfrey bought a 10 percent stake in Weight Watchers, an investment of $40 million. In one of her many commercials for the brand, she says, 'Let's make this the year of our best body.' The implication is, of course, that our current bodies are not our best bodies, not by a long shot. It is startling to realize that even Oprah, a woman in her early sixties, a billionaire and one of the most famous women in the world, isn't happy with herself, her body. That is how pervasive damaging cultural messages about unruly bodies are – that even as we age, no matter what material successes we achieve, we cannot be satisfied or happy unless we are also thin.

There is the commercial where Oprah glows as she tells us she has eaten bread every day in 2016, and still the world continues to turn. Or the commercial where she shouts, 'I love chips!' There is the commercial where she is cooking and crowing about all the pasta she gets to eat. By the grace of Weight Watchers, she is able to control her body and enjoy carbohydrates. There is the inspirational commercial where she boasts of having lost forty pounds, which, I imagine, means that finally she is living her best life.

In yet another commercial, Oprah somberly says, 'Inside every overweight woman is a woman she knows she can be.' This is a popular notion, the idea that the fat among us are carrying a thin woman inside. Each time I see this particular commercial, I think, *I ate that thin woman and she was delicious but unsatisfying.* And then I think about how fucked up it is to promote this idea that our truest selves are thin women hiding in our fat bodies like imposters, usurpers, illegitimates.

In this same commercial, Oprah goes on to talk

about how weight problems are never just weight problems, that there is often more to the story. This is often indeed true, but self-actualization, the catharsis of confronting demons is not what Oprah is truly selling. Instead, she is telling us that our ultimate goal is this better (th)inner woman we're supposed to diet toward. We will have our better body, and her empire will continue to grow.

CHAPTER 38

Gossip magazines keep us constantly abreast of what's happening to the bodies of famous women, the better to keep the rest of us in line. The weight fluctuations of famous women are tracked like stocks because their bodies are, in their line of work, their personal stock, the physical embodiment of market value. When a celebrity loses weight she is often billed as 'flaunting' her new body, which is, in fact, the only body she has ever had, but at a size more acceptable to the tabloids. When celebrity women have babies, their bodies are intensely monitored during and after – from baby bumps to post-baby bodies. After a celebrity has a baby, her size is assiduously tracked and documented until she once again resembles the extraordinarily thin woman we once knew.

Celebrity bodies provide the unachievable standard toward which we must nonetheless strive. They are *thinspiration* – thin inspiration – a constant reminder of the distance between our bodies and what our bodies could be with the proper discipline.

Celebrities understand the economy of thinness, and most of them are willing to participate in that economy, taking to social media, where they pose for selfies with their cheeks sucked in to make themselves appear even gaunter. The less space they take up, the more they matter.

CHAPTER 39

There is a taxonomy for the unruly, overweight human body, and that taxonomy becomes even more specific for the unruly overweight woman's body. As a fat woman, I have become intimately familiar with this taxonomy because this is the vernacular with which far too many people discuss my body and its parts.

In the culture at large, fat women can be many things in polite company – BBW (a big beautiful woman) or a SSBBW (super-sized big beautiful woman). She can be round, curvy, chubby, rotund, pleasantly plump, 'healthy,' heavy, heavyset, stout, husky, or thick. In impolite company a fat woman can be a pig, fat pig, cow, snow cow, fatty, blimp, blob, lard ass, tub of lard, fat ass, hog, beast, fatso, buffalo, whale, elephant, two tons of fun, and a slew of names I don't have the heart to share.

When it comes to our clothing, we have plus-sized clothing or extended sizes or queen sizes or 'women's' wear.

Specific body parts, 'problem areas,' also get labels – fupa, gunt, cankles, thunder thighs, Hi Susans, wings, cottage cheese thighs, hail damage, muffin tops, side boob, back fat, love handles, saddlebags, spare tires, double chins, gocks, man boobs, beer bellies.

These terms – the clinical, the casual, the slang, the insulting – are all designed to remind fat people that our bodies are not normal. Our bodies are so problematic as to have specific designations. It's a hell of a thing to have our bodies so ruthlessly, publicly dissected, defined, and denigrated.

CHAPTER 40

Part of disciplining the body is denial. We want but we dare not have. We deny ourselves certain foods. We deny ourselves rest by working out. We deny ourselves peace of mind by remaining ever vigilant over our bodies. We withhold from ourselves until we achieve a goal and then we withhold from ourselves to maintain that goal.

My body is wildly undisciplined, and yet I deny myself nearly everything I desire. I deny myself the right to space when I am in public, trying to fold in on myself, to make my body invisible even though it is, in fact, grandly visible. I deny myself the right to a shared armrest because how dare I impose? I deny myself entry into certain spaces I have deemed inappropriate for a body like mine – most spaces inhabited by other people, public transportation, anywhere I could be seen or where I might be in the way, really. I deny myself bright colors in my daily clothing choices, sticking to a uniform of denim and dark shirts even though I have a far more diverse wardrobe. I deny myself certain trappings of femininity as if I do not have the right to such expression when my body does not follow society's dictates for what a woman's body should look like. I deny myself gentler kinds of affection – to touch or be kindly touched – as if that is a pleasure a body like mine does not deserve. Punishment is, in fact, one of the few things I allow myself. I deny myself my attractions. I have them, oh I do, but dare not express them, because how dare I want. How dare I confess my want? How dare I try to act on that want? I deny myself so much, and still there is so much desire throbbing beneath my surfaces.

Denial merely puts what we want just beyond reach, but we still know it's there.

On a visit to Los Angeles, my best friend and I were drinking wine in a hotel room. During a pleasant lull in the conversation, she grabbed my hand to paint my thumbnail. She had been threatening to do this for hours and I was resisting for reasons I could not articulate. Finally, I surrendered and my hand was soft in hers as she carefully covered my nail in a lovely shade of pink. She blew on it, let it dry, added a second coat. The evening continued. I stared at my finger the next day as I sat on an airplane hurtling across the country. I could not remember the last time I had allowed myself the simple pleasure of a painted fingernail. I liked seeing my finger like that, particularly because my nail was long, nicely shaped, and I hadn't gnawed at it as I am wont to do. Then I became self-conscious and tucked my thumb against the palm of my hand, as if I should hide my thumb, as if I had no right to feel pretty, to feel good about myself, to acknowledge myself as a woman when I am clearly not following the rules for being a woman – to be small, to take up less space.

Before I got on the plane, my best friend offered me a bag of potato chips to eat on the plane, but I denied myself that. I told her, 'People like me don't get to eat food like that in public,' and it was one of the truest things I've ever said. Only the depth of our relationship allowed me to make this revelation and then I was ashamed for buying into these terrible narratives we fit ourselves into and I was ashamed at how I am so terrible about disciplining my body and I was ashamed by how I deny myself so much and it is still not enough.

CHAPTER 41

I hate myself. Or society tells me I am supposed to hate myself, so I guess this, at least, is something I am doing right.

Or, I should say, I hate my body. I hate my weakness at being unable to control my body. I hate how I feel in my body. I hate how people see my body. I hate how people stare at my body, treat my body, comment on my body. I hate equating my self-worth with the state of my body and how difficult it is to overcome this equation. I hate how hard it is to accept my human frailties. I hate that I am letting down so many women when I cannot embrace my body at any size.

But I also like myself, my personality, my weirdness, my sense of humor, my wild and deep romantic streak, how I love, how I write, my kindness and my mean streak. It is only now, in my forties, that I am able to admit that I like myself, even though I am nagged by this suspicion that I shouldn't. For so long, I gave in to my self-loathing. I refused to allow myself the simple pleasure of accepting who I am and how I live and love and think and see the world. But then, I got older and I cared less about what other people think. I got older and realized I was exhausted by all my self-loathing and that I was hating myself, in part, because I assumed that's what other people expected from me, as if my self-hatred was the price I needed to pay for living in an overweight body. It was much, much easier to just try and shut out all of that noise, and to try and forgive myself for the mistakes I made in high school and college and throughout my twenties, to have some empathy for why I made those mistakes.

I don't want to change who I am. I want to change how I look. On my better days, when I feel up to the fight, I want to change how this world responds to how I look because intellectually I know my body is not the real problem.

On bad days, though, I forget how to separate my personality, the heart of who I am, from my body. I forget how to shield myself from the cruelties of the world.

PART IV

CHAPTER 42

I hesitate to write about fat bodies and my fat body especially. I know that to be frank about my body makes some people uncomfortable. It makes me uncomfortable too. I have been accused of being full of self-loathing and of being fat-phobic. There is truth to the former accusation and I reject the latter. I do, however, live in a world where the open hatred of fat people is vigorously tolerated and encouraged. I am a product of my environment.

Oftentimes, the people who I make uncomfortable by admitting that I don't love being fat are what I like to call Lane Bryant fat. They can still buy clothes at stores like Lane Bryant, which offers sizes up to 26/28. They weigh 150 or 200 pounds less than I do. They know some of the challenges of being fat, but they don't know the challenges of being *very* fat.

To be clear, the fat acceptance movement is important, affirming, and profoundly necessary, but I also believe that part of fat acceptance is accepting that some of us struggle with body image and haven't reached a place of peace and unconditional self-acceptance.

I don't know where I fit in with communities of fat people. I'm aware of and regularly read about the Health at Every Size movement and other fat acceptance communities. I admire their work and their messages, find that work a necessary corrective to our culture's toxic attitudes toward women's bodies and fat bodies. I want to be embraced by these communities and their positivity. I want to know how they do it, how they find peace and self-acceptance.

I also want to lose weight. I know I am not healthy at this size (not because I am fat but because I have, for example, high blood pressure). More important, I am not happy at this size, though I am not suffering from the illusion that were I to wake up thin tomorrow, I would be happy and all my problems would be solved.

All things considered, I have a reasonable amount of self-esteem. When I'm around the right people, I feel strong and powerful and sexy. I am not fearless the way people assume I am, but despite all my fears, I am willing to take chances and I like that too about myself.

I hate how people treat and perceive me. I hate how I am extraordinarily visible but invisible. I hate not fitting in so many places where I want to be. I have it wired in my head that if I looked different this would change. Intellectually, I recognize the flaw in the logic, but emotionally, it's not so easy to make sense.

I want to have everything I need in my body

and I don't yet, but I will, I think. Or I will get closer. There are days when I am feeling braver. There are days when I am feeling, finally, like I can shed some of this protection I have amassed and be okay. I am not young but I am not old yet. I have a lot of life left, and my god, I want to do something different than what I have done for the last twenty years. I want to move freely. I want to be free.

CHAPTER 43

I am no stranger to dieting. I understand that, in general, to lose weight you need to eat less and move more. I can diet with reasonable success for months at a time. I restrict my calories and keep track of everything I eat. When I first started dieting under my parents' supervision, I would do this in paper journals. In this modern age, I use an app on my phone. I recognize that, despite what certain weight-loss system commercials would have me believe, I cannot eat everything and anything I want. And that is one of the cruelties of our cultural obsession with weight loss. We're supposed to restrict our eating while indulging in the fantasy that we can, indeed, indulge. It's infuriating. When you're trying to lose weight, you cannot have anything you want. That is, in fact, the whole point. Having anything you want is likely what contributed to your weight gain. Dieting requires deprivation, and it's easier when everyone faces that truth. When I am dieting, I try to face that truth, but I am not terribly successful.

There is always a moment when I am losing

weight when I feel better in my body. I breathe easier. I move better. I feel myself getting smaller and stronger. My clothes fall over my body the way they should and then they start to get baggy. I get terrified. I start to worry about my body becoming more vulnerable as it grows smaller. I start to imagine all the ways I could be hurt. I start to remember all the ways I have been hurt.

I also taste hope. I taste the idea of having more choices when I go clothes shopping. I taste the idea of fitting into seats at restaurants, movie theaters, waiting rooms. I taste the idea of walking into a crowded room or through a mall without being stared at and pointed at and talked about. I taste the idea of grocery shopping without strangers taking food they disapprove of out of my cart or offering me unsolicited nutrition advice. I taste the idea of being free of the realities of living in an overweight body. I taste the idea of being free.

And then I worry that I am getting ahead of myself. I worry that I won't be able to keep up better eating, more exercise, taking care of myself. Inevitably, I stumble and then I fall, and then I lose the taste of being free. I lose the taste of hope. I am left feeling low, like a failure. I am left feeling ravenously hungry and then I try to satisfy that hunger so I might undo all the progress I've made. And then I hunger even more.

CHAPTER 44

I start each day with the best of intentions for living a better, healthier life. Every morning, I wake up and have a few minutes where I am free from my body and my failings. During these moments, I think, *Today, I will make good choices. I will work out. I will eat small portions. I will take the stairs when possible.* Before the day starts, I am fully prepared to tackle the problem of my body, to be better than I have been. But then I get out of bed. Often, I rush to get ready and begin my day because I am not a morning person and I hit SNOOZE on my alarm several times. I don't eat breakfast because I'm not hungry or I don't have time or there is no food in the house, which are all excuses for not being willing to take proper care of myself. Sometimes, I eat lunch – a sandwich from Subway or Jimmy John's. Or two sandwiches. And chips. And a cookie or three. And it's fine, I tell myself, because I haven't eaten all day. Or I wait until dinner and then the day is nearly done and I can eat whatever I want, I tell myself, because I have not eaten all day.

At night, I have to face myself and all the ways

I have failed. Most days, I haven't exercised. I haven't made any of the good choices I intended to make when the day began. Whatever happens next doesn't matter, so I binge and eat even more of whatever I want. As I fall asleep, my stomach churning, the acids making my heartburn flare, I think about the next day. I think, *Tomorrow, I will make good choices.* I am always holding on to the hope of tomorrow.

CHAPTER 45

I often try to create goals for myself that go beyond what I hope to accomplish for my body in a given day. I will lose x number of pounds by the time I go home for Thanksgiving or Christmas or before I go to Australia or before I next see my loved one. I will lose x number of pounds before I go on book tour. I will lose x number of pounds before the new semester starts. I will lose x number of pounds before I go to the Beyoncé concert. I create these goals and make half-hearted attempts to meet these goals, but I never do, and then I enter a spiral of feeling like a failure for not ever being able to be better, to get smaller.

I reserve my most elaborate delusions and disappointments for myself.

CHAPTER 46

My disdain for sports and, now, exercise remains pure and constant. It feels like a waste of my time, moving around, sweating and hoping that something good will rise from that effort. Certainly, there are moments after a workout when I feel refreshed and powerful and healthy, but it is very easy to forget those moments when I need to change into workout clothes and go to the gym or go for a walk, or do whatever it takes to move my body.

I generally dread exercise, all of it, and then I feel terrible about myself for being lazy, unmotivated, utterly lacking in discipline or self-regard, because intellectually, I know exercise is good for me. My hatred of exercise is unfortunate because exercise is necessary for the human body. It is a key component of losing weight and good health. I know the math.

In order to maintain your body weight, you need to eat 11 calories for every pound you weigh. In order to lose a pound of fat, you must burn 3,500 calories. If you're a 150-pound woman, thirty minutes of aerobic exercise burns about

220 calories. Thirty minutes of elliptical training burns about 280 calories. Running at a brisk pace will burn 120 calories for each mile. A brisk walk will burn 100 calories for each mile. I should take some consolation in knowing that at my size, I burn way more calories than the 150-pound woman, but alas, I do not.

In the corner of my bedroom sits my recumbent exercise bike. When I am feeling particularly motivated about losing weight, I will ride the bike for up to an hour a day. It's a good time to sweat and catch up on reading. I own a few hand weights that I'll flex and curl when I remember to. I have a large inflatable ball upon which I sit to do abdominal exercises and squats and the like. I do not suffer from ignorance where exercise is related. I suffer from inertia.

Over the years, I have joined countless gyms. I have worked with personal trainers, though grudgingly, given that I hate being told what to do and that hatred multiplies when I am told what to do by someone who is thin and impossibly fit and usually gorgeous and charging me a significant amount of money on an hourly basis.

I have a membership to Planet Fitness, though I have never visited the local facility. Basically, I donate $19.99 a month to their corporate existence and the *idea* that I can walk into a Planet Fitness, anywhere in the country, should I feel like working out.

I have worked with personal trainers off and on

over the years, recognizing that perhaps the support of a professional might help me improve my physical fitness. These days, my trainer is a young guy born and raised in Indiana named Tijay. He is short and compact and has an unbelievable body. His whole life is fitness. He literally glows with youth, health, and the vigorous enthusiasm of having the world as his oyster. He is a big advocate of chicken breasts as a source of protein and mustard as an accompanying condiment because it is fat free and very low in calories. Not a session goes by when he doesn't mention some aspect of his diet that makes me so sad for him and his palate. I worry he doesn't know about spices or flavor or anything that makes food delicious.

Tijay never seems to know what to make of me because I do not glow and I am not young and I am not cheerful. He runs me through my paces, always offering me encouragement. He is not a nightmare trainer out to break my soul. He is genuine and kind and dedicated and I suppose I am his albatross. I am his project. He's just so cheerful. He is a true believer in the benefits of a 'healthy lifestyle.' He makes it all seem so easy, as I pant and sweat and ache. I want to murder this man when we work out. I am generally terrified I will drop dead at any moment, my heart pounding in my chest as I struggle to catch my breath. Sometimes, when he asks me to do something that seems well beyond my big body's abilities, I want to scream, 'Don't you see that I'm fat?' I once asked this very question and he said, very calmly, 'That's why we're here,' and I walked to my nearby water bottle, drank freely, muttering, 'Fuck you,' under my breath.

In truth, I curse at him frequently and he takes it all in stride. Each visit, he adds an exercise or intensifies an exercise we have previously done. Each visit, I stumble to my car with rubbery legs and wonder how I will find the strength to return. I sit in my car, sometimes for up to ten minutes, drenched in sweat, drinking water. I take selfies that I post to Snapchat with angry words about how much I hate exercise, and when I share these selfies on Twitter, people offer encouragement and advice, even though I am looking for neither. I am just sharing my suffering. I am looking for commiseration.

When I go to the gym on my own, I always feel like all eyes are on me. I try to pick times when there won't be many people around, partly to protect myself, partly out of self-loathing. My self-consciousness magnifies at the gym. There is something about actively using my body that makes me feel even more vulnerable. And there is, of course, the self-doubt, the nagging sense that I shouldn't even bother, that I don't belong in the gym, that any attempt toward fitness is pathetic and delusional.

I know how to use most of the equipment, but I always get nervous when I am mounting the treadmill or an exercise bike because I feel like that equipment isn't meant for people like me. I hate how other people will see me, this fat person working out, and offer unsolicited encouragement like, 'Good for you,' or 'Keep it up,' or 'You go, girl.' I don't want encouragement. I am not interested in anyone's opinions about my presence in the gym. I do not require the affirmation of strangers. Those affirmations are rarely about genuine encouragement or kindness. They are an expression of the fear of unruly bodies. They are a misguided attempt to reward the behavior of a 'good fat person,' who is, in their minds, trying to lose weight rather than simply engaging in healthful behavior.

When I am at the gym, I want to be left alone in my sweaty misery. I want to disappear until my body is no longer a spectacle. I can't disappear, though, so either I have to be graceful in the face of this unsolicited conversation or I have to ignore it because, if I allowed myself to lose control, I would let loose so much rage.

CHAPTER 47

This one time, many years ago, I went to the gym and five of the six recumbent bikes, my equipment of choice, were occupied by gorgeous, extraordinarily thin women, predominantly of the blond persuasion, who arrived and staked their claim just before I did. I looked around, wondering if a movie was being filmed or if it was Sorority Workout Hour. I was unable to deduce the exact reason why these young women were in the gym at the very time I chose to exercise, but it was clear they were working out together. I became irritated and downright angry as I always do when I see exceedingly thin people at the gym. It doesn't matter that they are most likely thin for this very reason. I feel like they are mocking me with their perfect, toned bodies. They are flaunting their physical blessings and discipline.

There is a smugness to how they use the exercise equipment, programming the computers for the most challenging levels. Their placid facial expressions say, 'This is hardly bothering me,' their bodies glowing with a thin patina of perspiration rather than the gritty sweat of serious exertion.

They wear their cute little outfits – shorts so short that the material is more a suggestion than an actual item of clothing and narrow tank tops with the scooped shoulders designed to reveal as much surface area of their perfect bodies as possible. They know that they work hard and look good and they want everyone else to know it too.

On that day, I was forced to use the bike I hate the most – the one closest to the entrance to the cardio/weight room, so that my sweating and huffing and puffing and personal tics would be on display for each and every person coming and going through the adjacent doors. I settled in, programmed the machine for sixty minutes, knowing I would stop at forty but giving myself some room to push myself if I wasn't dying by then. I glanced over at the girl next to me. She had been on the bike for about two minutes longer. When forty minutes passed, my legs were burning fiercely. I looked at my neighbor and she looked back at me. She had been eyeing me the entire time, wondering just how long I was going to last.

After forty-five minutes, I locked eyes with my neighbor/nemesis again and saw a glint in her eyes. I knew what was going on. She was challenging me. She was letting me know that however long I lasted, she would last longer. She would not be bested by a fat ass. At fifty minutes, I was certain that a heart attack was imminent. I was dizzy, faint, legs trembling, but death was preferable to losing to that young upstart, that hussy. At fifty-three minutes, she glared at me, leaned forward, and grabbed the handles of the bike. I turned up the volume on my music and started bobbing my head to the beat. At fifty-four minutes, she grunted and tried to stare through me. Finally, she stopped and I heard her say, 'I can't believe she's still on there.' Her friends nodded in agreement. At sixty minutes, I calmly stopped pedaling, peeled my shirt away from my skin, wiped the bike down, and slowly exited the room because my legs were rubbery and weak. I was trying to project poise and strength. I knew *she* was watching. I was smug and temporarily triumphant. Then I stepped into the bathroom and threw up, ignoring the bitter taste at the back of my throat as I embraced a hollow victory.

CHAPTER 48

I have many athletic friends, and because I am active on social media, I often see them posting pictures of their physical accomplishments. They wear their shorts and Under Armour shirts, molded to their incredibly fit bodies; their hair, damp with sweat, is plastered to their faces. They hold race numbers triumphantly in the air. They proudly display medals from finishing 5Ks and 10Ks and half marathons and whole marathons and sometimes races that are even more absurd, like Tough Mudders and triathlons and ultramarathons. They use apps that post athletic progress to Facebook and Twitter: 'I ran 6.24 miles.' 'I biked 24.5 miles.' Or they personally post a little update: 'Just climbed a mountain and enjoyed a picnic from the summit.' The pictures accompanying these updates reveal people glowing with health and vigor.

They are, rightly, proud of what they have done with their bodies, but when I am at my pettiest, which is often, it feels like gloating. Or, if I am being honest, they are bragging about something I might never know, that kind of personal satisfaction with and sense of accomplishment provided by my body. I get angry as I see these updates because these people are doing things I cannot. They are doing things I hope, so very much want, to someday be able to do in theory, even if I won't actually do them given that I am not at all interested in sports or the outdoors. I am not angry. I am jealous. I am seething with jealousy. I want to be part of the active world. I want it so very badly. There are so many things I hunger for.

CHAPTER 49

I am self-conscious beyond measure. I am intensely and constantly preoccupied with my body in the world because I know what people think and what they see when they look at me. I know that I am breaking the unspoken rules of what a woman should look like.

I am hyperconscious of how I take up space. As a woman, as a fat woman, I am not supposed to take up space. And yet, as a feminist, I am encouraged to believe I *can* take up space. I live in a contradictory space where I should try to take up space but not too much of it, and not in the wrong way, where the wrong way is any way where my body is concerned. Whenever I am near other people, I try to fold into myself so that my body doesn't disrupt the space of others. I take this to extremes. I will spend five-hour flights tucked against the window, my arm tucked into the seat belt, as if trying to create absence where there is excessive presence. I walk at the edge of sidewalks. In buildings I hug the walls. I try to walk as quickly as I can when I feel someone behind me so I don't get in their way, as if I have less of a right to be in the world than anyone else.

I am hyperconscious of how I take up space and I resent having to be this way, so when people around me aren't mindful of how they take up space, I feel pure rage. I am seething with jealousy. I hate that they don't have to consider how they take up space. They can walk at any speed they want. Their limbs can spill over armrests. They can dawdle and stretch and shrug, no matter where they are. I rage that they don't have to second-guess themselves or give a moment's thought to the space they fill. The ease with which they take up space feels spiteful and personal.

I am, perhaps, self-obsessed beyond measure. No matter where I am, I wonder about where I stand and how I look. I think, *I am the fattest person in this apartment building. I am the fattest person in this class. I am the fattest person at this university. I am the fattest person in this theater. I am the fattest person on this airplane. I am the fattest person in this airport. I am the fattest person on this interstate. I am the fattest person in this city. I am the fattest person at this event. I am the fattest person at this conference. I am the fattest person in this restaurant. I am the fattest person in this shopping mall. I am the fattest person on this panel. I am the fattest person in this casino.*

I am the fattest person.

This is a constant, destructive refrain and I cannot escape it.

CHAPTER 50

I am terrified of other people. I am terrified of the way they are likely to look at me, stare, talk about me or say cruel things to me. I am terrified of children, their guilelessness and brutal honesty and willingness to gawk at me, to talk loudly about me, to ask their parents or, sometimes, even me, 'Why are you so big?' I am terrified of the awkward pause of those children's parents as they try to respond appropriately.

I do not have an answer to that question, or I do and there simply isn't enough time or grace in the world to offer that answer up.

And so I am terrified of other people. I hear the rude comments whispered. I see the stares and laughs and snickering. I see the thinly veiled or open disgust. I pretend I don't see it. I block it out as often as I can so I can live and breathe with some semblance of peace. The list of bullshit I deal with, by virtue of my body, is long and boring, and I am, frankly, bored with it. This is the world we live in. Looks matter, and we can say, 'But but but . . .' But no. Looks matter. Bodies matter.

I could easily become a shut-in, hiding from

the cruelty of the world. Most days it takes all my strength and no small amount of courage to get dressed and leave the house. If I don't have to teach or travel for work, I spend most of my time talking myself out of leaving my house. I can order something in. I can make do with what I have. *Tomorrow*, I promise myself. *Tomorrow I will face the world.* If it's late in the week, there are several tomorrows until Monday. There are several tomorrows when I can lie to myself, when I can hope to build stronger defenses for facing the world that so cruelly faces me.

CHAPTER 51

I have two wardrobes. One, the clothes I wear every day, is made up mostly of dark denim jeans, black T-shirts, and, for special occasions, dress shirts. These clothes shroud my cowardice. These are the clothes I feel safe in. This is the armor I wear to face the world, and I assure you, armor is needed. I tell myself this armor is all I need. When I wear my typical uniform, it feels like safety, like I can hide in plain sight. I become less of a target. I am taking up space, but I am doing so in an unassuming manner so I am less of a problem, less of a disturbance. This is what I tell myself.

My other wardrobe, the one that dominates most of my closet, is full of the clothes I don't have the courage to wear.

I am nowhere near as brave as people believe me to be. As a writer, armed with words, I can do anything, but when I have to take my body out into the world, courage fails me.

I am fat. I am six foot three. I take up space in nearly every way. I stand out when my nature is to very much want to disappear.

But I love fashion. I love the idea of wearing color, blouses with interesting cuts and silhouettes, something low-cut that shows off my décolletage. I have any number of fine dress slacks, and I enjoy staring at them in my closet, so sleek and professional, so unlike me. I dream of wearing a long skirt or a maxi dress with bold, bright stripes. My breath catches at the mere thought of wearing something sleeveless, baring my brown arms. Fierce vanity smolders in the cave of my chest. I want to look good. I want to feel good. I want to be beautiful in this body I am in.

The story of my life is wanting, hungering, for what I cannot have or, perhaps, wanting what I dare not allow myself to have.

Many mornings, most mornings, I stand in my closet, trying to figure out what I am going to wear for the day. Really, this is part of an elaborate, exhausting performance in which the end result is always the same. But I have my delusions and I entertain them with alarming frequency and vigor. I try on various outfits and marvel at all the cute clothes I own. If I am feeling particularly brave, I take a look at myself in the mirror. It's always surprising to see myself out of my usual clothes, to see how my body looks shrouded in color or something other than denim and cotton.

Sometimes, I decide on an outfit and leave my bedroom. It's a mundane moment, but for me, it is not. I decide, *Today, I am a professional and I will look the part.* I make breakfast, or get my things together for work. I feel strange and awkward. In a matter of moments, it begins to feel like these unfamiliar clothes are strangling me. I see and feel every unflattering bulge and curve. My throat constricts. I can't breathe. The clothes shrink. Sleeves become tourniquets. Slacks become shackles. I start to panic, and before I know it, I am tearing the bright, beautiful clothes off because I don't deserve to wear them.

When I slide back into my uniform, that cloak of safety returns. I can breathe again. And then I start to hate myself for my unruly body that I seem incapable of disciplining, for my cowardice in the face of what other people might think.

CHAPTER 52

Sometimes people try to offer me fashion advice. They say there is so much out there for big girls. But they're thinking about a very specific kind of big girl. There is very little out there for a very big girl like me.

Buying clothes is an ordeal. It is but one of many humiliations fat people endure. I hate clothes shopping and have for years because I know I'm not going to find anything I actually want to wear. We hear the statistics about how obesity is a major problem in the United States, and yet there are a mere handful of stores where fat people can buy clothes. At most of those stores, the clothes are hideous.

Generally, we can go to Lane Bryant, the Avenue, Catherines. Other stores – Maurices, Old Navy, various department stores – offer a small selection of plus-sized clothing. There are online purveyors of plus-sized clothing, but they are hit-or-miss. And there is this – most of these stores have nothing to offer for the super morbidly obese. Lane Bryant's sizes generally go to 28, and the same goes for most other stores. The Avenue, more generously, offers clothing up to size 32. If you are larger than that, and I am larger than that, there are so very few options. Being fashionable is not among them.

There is also the option of wearing men's clothes, and sometimes I do. Men have a few more choices in that larger sizes are often carried in department stores. Still, there are relatively few offerings, and in recent years, they've all been consolidated under the Casual Male/Destination XL banner.

During my twenties, I preferred men's clothing because I could hide my femininity, feeling it made me safer. But men's clothes are often ill-fitting. They are not designed and constructed to accommodate breasts and curves and hips. They are not designed to make a girl feel pretty.

With so few clothing options available to me, I am full of longing. There is so much I don't get to do. There are no fun shopping trips to the mall. There is no sharing clothes with friends. My person can't really buy me clothes as a gift. I flip through fashion magazines and covet what I see, while knowing that such beauty is, for now, beyond my reach. These are trivial wants but they aren't.

In the big cities I frequent, mostly New York and Los Angeles, I become increasingly aware of my lack of style as impeccably dressed people surround me wearing the kinds of clothing I would love to wear, if only . . .

I rarely feel attractive or sexy or well dressed. I hardly know what it feels like to wear something

I truly want or like. If I find something that fits, I buy it because there is so little that fits. I don't like patterns. I don't like appliqué. Fat-girl clothes designers never got this memo.

I am angry that the fashion industry is completely unwilling to design for a more diverse range of human bodies.

In my teens and early twenties, I often went clothes shopping with my mother and I could always see her dismay at where I am forced to shop. I could see that she wished her daughter had a different body. I could see her humiliation and frustration. Sometimes, she told me, 'I hope this is the last time we have to shop here,' and I murmured my agreement. I harbored the same hope. I also knew it wouldn't be the last time. I harbored no small amount of frustration, or anger, for her words, for her disappointment in me, for my inability to be a good daughter, for one more thing I couldn't have – the simple pleasure of having fun while shopping with my mother.

A couple years ago, I was in a clothing store, alone. I wanted to find a few nice things to wear. I wanted to look nice for someone who loves me exactly as I am and who makes me care about my appearance and who has taught me to care about myself in ways both great and small. Wanting to look nice for someone was new and I liked it.

I was at this store, looking for some cute, colorful shirts, when a young woman came out of the dressing room crying. The details aren't mine to share but she was so upset and her mother was treating her in quite a humiliating manner and I wanted to sob right there in the store because it was just too much to see such a familiar and painful scene. Fat daughters and their thin mothers have especially complicated relationships.

I've been that girl, too big for the clothes in the store, just trying to find something, anything, that fits, while also dealing with the commentary of someone else who means well but can't help but make pointed, insensitive comments. To be that girl in a clothing store is to be the loneliest girl in the world.

I am not a hugger, but I wanted to wrap my arms around this girl. I wanted to protect her from this world that is so unbelievably cruel to overweight people. There was nothing I could really do because I know this world. I live in it too. There's no shelter or safety or escape from the cruel stares and comments, the too-small seats, the too-small every-thing for your too-big body.

But I followed her to the dressing room and I told her she was beautiful. And she was indeed beautiful. She nodded, tears were streaming down her face. We both went on with our shopping. I wanted to tear her mother's face off. I wanted to call my person and hear a kind voice. I wanted something to pull me out of the spiral of self-loathing I felt myself tumbling into. I wanted to burn the store down. I wanted to scream.

When the young woman left the store with her

mother, she was still crying. I cannot stop picturing her face, that look in her eyes that I know too well, how she was trying to fold in on herself in a body that was so visible. She was trying to disappear and she couldn't. It is unbearable to want something so little and need it so much.

CHAPTER 53

I never imagined myself to be the kind of person who got a tattoo. They were certainly frowned upon by my family as a mark of criminality, at best. But in the after, I wasn't a good girl and I didn't have to follow the rules as I once knew them. My parents, I knew, would freak out because they were still holding on to the idea of who they thought I was. But my getting a tattoo was not about them. It was about me doing something I wanted, that I chose, to my body.

And so I got my first tattoo when I was nineteen. I started with a woman with wings. The artist said getting the tattoo would hurt as he wiped my arm with rubbing alcohol, swiped a plastic razor over the hairs, removing them from his flesh canvas. I waited for pain but I felt nothing. I sat quietly and watched as the ink seeped into my skin. When I look at the arcs of ink, more than twenty years later, I still see a woman with wings, a woman who can escape anything she wants, even her body.

I got my next tattoo not long after, a tribal design, black and red, just below the first tattoo on my left forearm. I wish I could say I had some kind of thoughtful approach to my tattoos, but I didn't. I just wanted to have control over (the marking of) my body.

I recognize the inherent tension in my getting tattoos while also wanting to be invisible. People notice tattoos. My tattoos often inspire conversation. People ask me about the significance or meaning of my tattoos and I don't have good answers. Or, rather, I don't have the kinds of answers people want to hear: convenient, easy ones.

My first few tattoos were small, tentative. With each successive one, the ink has gotten bigger, spread wider across my skin. I love the act of getting a tattoo. It's not so much about the design as it is the experience of being marked. I love watching the artist set up the workspace, ink, needles, razor.

With my tattoos, I get to say, these are choices I make for my body, with full-throated consent. This is how I mark myself. This is how I take my body back.

While I was in Lake Tahoe in 2014, teaching at a brief residency MFA program, I got a new tattoo, my first one in years. Before I got that tattoo, I was sitting at a fire by a lake with the writers Colum McCann, Josh Weil, and Randa Jarrar. This isn't name-dropping. That is simply who was there because we were all teaching in the same program. Colum asked me, 'So why the tattoos?' with his lilting accent and bright eyes. This is a question I get asked a lot. It's a bit invasive, but you invite such invasion when you mark yourself openly with dark ink. People want to know why. We want to transgress boundaries. I include myself in this. I don't think we can help it. I told Colum a version of the truth of why I mark my body like this, about what it means to have at least some measure of control over my skin.

Here, in the middle of my life, I would do things differently if I had to do it all again, but I would still have tattoos.

Now and again, I get the urge for a new tattoo. I get the urge to feel connected to my body in a way I am rarely allowed. I get the urge to be touched in that very specific way, the artist holding some part of my body, their hand sheathed in latex while they use this tool, this weapon really, forcing a series of needles into my skin over and over again, the pliant flesh becoming more and more tender.

There is a certain amount of submission in receiving a tattoo, so of course I'm very much into that controlled surrender. I love the submission of turning my body over to this stranger for hours. I love the pain, which isn't excruciating but is incredibly, infuriatingly persistent, accompanied by the endless whine of the tattoo gun, marking me forever. This guy who tattooed me in Tahoe was all about asserting his dominance. He made it clear that he was an alpha male. As he worked me over, he literally said, 'I am an alpha male,' and it took all my self-control not to roll my eyes.

During a tattoo, pain is constant and sometimes

it lasts hours, but it doesn't necessarily register the same way pain normally does. I am not to be trusted on this. I do not register pain as most people do, which is to say, my tolerance is high. It is probably too high. But the pain of a tattoo is something to which you have to surrender because once you've started, you cannot really go back or you'll be left with something not only permanent but unfinished. I enjoy the irrevocability of that circumstance. You have to allow yourself this pain. You have chosen this suffering, and at the end of it, your body will be different. Maybe your body will feel more like yours.

I'm overweight. I hope to not always be, but for now, this is my body. I am coming to terms with that. I am trying to feel less shame about that. When I mark myself with ink, or when I have that done to me, I am taking some part of my skin back. It is a long, slow process. This is my fortress.

CHAPTER 54

To tell the story of my body is to tell you about shame – being ashamed of how I look, ashamed of my weakness, the shame of knowing it is in my power to change my body and yet, year after year, not changing it. Or I try, I do. I eat right. I work out. My body becomes smaller and starts to feel more like mine and not a cage of flesh I carry with me. That's when I feel a new kind of panic because I am seen in a different way. My body becomes a different source of discussion. I have more wardrobe options and there is that intoxicating moment when a much smaller pair of pants slips over my body and a shirt drapes easily over my shoulders. The vanity nestled in the cave of my chest swells.

In such moments, I see myself in the mirror, narrower, more angular. I recognize the me I could have, should have, would have been and want to be. That version of myself is terrifying and maybe even beautiful, so I panic, and within days or weeks, I undo all the progress I've made. I stop going to the gym. I stop eating right. I do this until I feel safe again.

Most of us have these versions of ourselves that terrify us. We have these imperfect bodies we don't quite know how to cope with. We have these shames we keep to ourselves because to show ourselves as we are, no more and no less, would be too much.

Shame is a difficult thing. People certainly try to shame me for being fat. When I am walking down the street, men lean out of their car windows and shout vulgar things at me about my body, how they see it, and how it upsets them that I am not catering to their gaze and their preferences and desires. I try not to take these men seriously because what they are really saying is, 'I am not attracted to you. I do not want to fuck you, and this confuses my understanding of my masculinity, entitlement, and place in this world.' It is not my job to please them with my body.

It is, however, difficult to hold on to what I know in the face of what I feel when I am reminded so publicly, so violently, of how certain people see me. It is difficult to not feel like I am the problem, and like I should do whatever it takes to make sure I don't compel such men to taunt me in the future.

Fat shaming is real, constant, and rather pointed. There are a shocking number of people who believe they can simply torment fat people into weight loss and disciplining their bodies or disappearing their bodies from the public sphere. They believe they are medical experts, listing a litany of

190

health problems associated with fatness as personal affronts. These tormentors bind themselves in righteousness when they point out the obvious – that our bodies are unruly, defiant, fat. It's a strange civic-minded cruelty. When people try to shame me for being fat, I feel rage. I get stubborn. I want to make myself fatter to spite the shamers, even though the only person I would really be spiting is myself.

CHAPTER 55

I am full of longing and I am full of envy and so much of my envy is terrible. I watch a *Nightline* special – an exposé on the horrors of eating disorders. I am morbidly fascinated by such programs and their human subjects. There is something about the gaunt faces and sharply angled bodies of anorexic girls that at once attracts and repulses me. I wonder what holds their bodies together. I envy the way their flesh is stretched taut against their brittle bones. I envy the way their clothes hang listlessly from their bodies, as if they aren't even being worn but, rather, floating – a veritable vestment halo rewarding their thinness. The reporter speaks with disdain about the rigorous exercise regimens these girls put themselves through, the starvation, the obsession with their bodies. And still, I am envious because these girls have willpower. They have the commitment to do what it takes to have the bodies they want. I ignore their thinning hair, rotting teeth, internal organs dissolving into mushy nothing. I prefer, instead, to obsess over their bodies the way others obsess over mine. I tell myself that soon, I am going to be that girl who eats a saltine cracker and says she's full. I will be that girl who spends hours at the gym, draped in oversized clothing. I will be the girl carefully purging unnecessary calories from her body with a well-placed finger down the throat. I will be the girl everyone loves to hate to love as my teeth yellow and my hair falls out but my body finally begins to become more acceptable, until my body withers and then disappears, stops taking up space.

Somehow, I never become that girl. And then I hate myself for wanting something so terrible and I rage at the world that hates me for my body and how it is so markedly visible and the same world that forces too many girls and women to try their best to disappear. My rage is often silent because no one wants to hear fat-girl stories of taking up too much space and still finding nowhere to fit. People prefer the stories of the too-skinny girls who starve themselves and exercise too much and are gray and gaunt and disappearing in plain sight.

CHAPTER 56

I often feel ravenous even if I am not hungry. On bad days, and I have many bad days, I eat a lot. I tell myself I don't do this. I tell myself that I'm not sitting around eating candy or Cheetos all day. That's true. I don't keep junk food at home. I don't make a habit of eating junk food. But then I become fixated on a certain food and then I eat it and eat it and eat it for days on end, sometimes weeks, until I am sick of it. It is a compulsion, I suppose.

When I am eating a meal, I have no sense of portion control. I am a completist. If the food is on my plate, I must finish it. If there is food left on the stove, I must finish it. Rarely do I have leftovers. At first, it feels good, savoring each bite, the world falling away. I forget about my stresses, my sadness. All I care about are the flavors in my mouth, the extraordinary pleasure of the act of eating. I start to feel full but I ignore that fullness and then that sense of fullness goes away and all I feel is sick, but still, I eat. When there is nothing left, I no longer feel comfort. What I feel is guilt and uncontrollable self-loathing, and oftentimes,

I find something else to eat, to soothe those feelings and, strangely, to punish myself, to make myself feel sicker so that the next time, I might remember how low I feel when I overindulge.

I never remember.

This is to say, I know what it means to hunger without being hungry. My father believes hunger is in the mind. I know differently. I know that hunger is in the mind and the body and the heart and the soul.

CHAPTER 57

I have chronic heartburn because I used to make myself throw up after I ate. There's a word for this, 'bulimia,' but it always feels strange to use that word with regard to myself. For a time, I did try to become that girl I envy, the one with the discipline to disorder her eating. I didn't do it for that long, I tell myself. That's not really the truth. I did it for about two years, which isn't that long but is long enough. Or, maybe I don't want to use the word because it was so long ago, which is absolutely not the truth. I stopped making myself throw up about four years ago. And sometimes, I relapse. Sometimes, I just want to rid myself of all the food in my body. I want to feel empty.

Once upon a time, I began to purge because I wanted to feel empty. I wanted to feel empty but I also wanted to fill myself. I was not a teenager or even in my twenties. I was in my thirties, and finally, I found the discipline to have an eating disorder. That first night, I wanted a huge rib eye steak, medium rare, over cold lettuce topped with salad dressing, croutons, and cheese. I found two thick cuts of rib eye at the grocery store, nicely marbled. I bought a package of Double Stuf Oreos. Like a thoroughly modern woman I consulted the Internet. I took that time to learn how to binge and purge and was both fascinated and appalled at the information I found. I learned that it helps to drink a lot of water right before you purge and that at the beginning of your binge you should eat carrots so you have a visual marker of when you've rid yourself of everything you've eaten. I learned that chocolate tastes the worst as it comes back up (and this would end up being absolutely true). I learned that my fingers might get cut from my teeth and that stomach acid would burn my knuckles (and these things were also true).

When I felt sufficiently prepared, I made my dinner and enjoyed a rush of excitement at the prospect of being able to eat whatever I wanted without consequence. This, I assured myself, was the dream. I ate all of that food, the steaks, the huge salad, the package of cookies. My stomach ached and I felt bloated and nauseated in a way I had never felt before. I didn't want to wait too long, so I rushed to my kitchen sink, gulped down three glasses of water, and stared into the aluminum basin as I shoved two fingers down my throat. It took a few jabs, but soon, I started gagging. My eyes watered. And then I was heaving and vomiting all that food I had just eaten. When I was done, I turned on the water and the disposal and all evidence of what I had done slowly disappeared.

For once, I did not feel shame after eating. I felt incredible. I felt in control. I wondered why it had taken me so long to try purging.

When you're fat, no one will pay attention to disordered eating or they will look the other way or they will look right through you. You get to hide in plain sight. I have hidden in plain sight, in one way or another, for most of my life. Willing myself to not do that anymore, willing myself to be seen, is difficult.

I was not fat and then I made myself fat. I needed my body to be a hulking, impermeable mass. I wasn't like other girls, I told myself. I got to eat everything I wanted and everything they wanted too. I was so free. I was free, in a prison of my own making.

I got older and I kept eating mostly just to keep the prison walls up. It was more work than you might imagine. Then I was in a great relationship with a great man and I was finishing my PhD and my life was coming together and I thought I could see a way out of the prison I had made.

We suffered a loss and it undid me. I needed to blame something or someone, so I blamed myself. I blamed my body for being broken. My doctor did not dissuade me from doing this, which was its own kind of hell – to have your worst fear about yourself affirmed by a medical professional who is credentialed to make such judgments.

My body was to blame. I was to blame. I needed to change my body but I also wanted to eat because eating was a comfort and I needed comfort but refused to ask the one person who could comfort me for such sanctuary. This was something I had long known so well. Before that point, I had often joked that I wasn't bulimic because I couldn't make myself throw up, but when I really want to do something, I get it done. I learned how to make myself throw up and then I got very good at it.

I am fat, so I hid in plain sight, eating, throwing up, eating. I am perfectly normal and fine, I told myself. One day, my boyfriend found me in the bathroom, hunched over the toilet, my eyes red and watering. It was a nasty scene. 'Get the fuck out,' I said quietly. I hadn't said more than a few words to him, to anyone, in months.

He grabbed me and pulled me to my feet. He shook me and said, 'This is what you're doing? This?' I just stared at him because I knew that would make him angrier. I wanted to make him angrier so that he could punish me and I could stop punishing myself. He deserved to punish me and I wanted to give that to him as penance. He was, is, a good man, so he wouldn't give me what I wanted. He uncurled his fingers and let go of me and backed out of the bathroom. He put his fist through a wall, which only infuriated me because I wanted him to put his fist through me.

After that, he tried to never leave me alone. He tried to save me from myself. Ha! Ha! Ha! I'm better, I told him. I'm done with all that, I told him. I was better, I suppose. I was better about hiding what I was doing. He couldn't follow me everywhere. I learned how to be very quiet. We were better, or as better as we ever were going to be, and then I graduated and I moved and he didn't follow and I was finally living alone and I could do whatever I wanted. I was an accomplished professional, so it was easier than ever to hide in plain sight.

In the new town no one really knew me. I had 'friends,' but it's not like they came over to my apartment or had gotten to know me well enough to see that anything was off. When we'd go out to dinner, friends remarked that I always went to the bathroom after I ate. 'I have a bad stomach,' I demurred, politely. It was a half-truth.

Immediately, I was extraordinarily on the rebound, involved with a guy. The one time he caught me throwing up he said, 'I'm glad you're working on the problem.' For him, the real problem was my body, and he never let me forget it. He punished me and I liked it. Finally, I thought. Finally. He made his cruel comments and gave me 'advice,' which only reminded me that everything wrong with my body was, indeed, my fault. 'Why are you with this asshole?' so many people – friends, strangers who saw us together in public – asked. The longer I stayed with him, the worse he made me feel, and the better he made me feel because, at last, someone was telling me a truth about myself I already knew.

Something had to give. Something always gives.

My grief began to subside. I was way too old for this shit, I realized. The heartburn had started up and I realized I needed to stop punishing myself. I had finally, after more than thirty years, found a best friend who saw the best and worst parts of me, and even if I didn't talk about what was going on, she was there and I could have told her and it would have been fine. That's a powerful thing, knowing you can reveal yourself to someone. It made me want to be a better person.

I wanted to stop, but wanting and doing are two different things. I had a routine. I starved myself all day and then I ate a huge meal and then I purged myself of that meal. I made myself empty and I loved that empty feeling. I ignored my yellowed teeth and my hair falling out and the acid burns on my right fingers and the scabs on my knuckles. 'Why is my hair falling out?' I asked the Internet, as if I didn't already know.

The truth was more complicated and I didn't know how to share it. I didn't think anyone in my life would even care about the truth so long as I was dealing with my body by any means necessary. We have to worry about the emaciated girls being fed through a tube in the nose, not girls like me. And also, I was really so old to be dealing with what we think of as an adolescent problem. I was embarrassed. I am embarrassed. You can't look up to me. I'm a fucking mess.

I became a vegetarian because I needed a way of ordering my eating that was less harmful. I needed something to focus on that didn't involve bringing my guts up every day. I thought I would only be a vegetarian for a year, but it ended up sticking for nearly four years, until I became too anemic and had to start eating meat again.

The word 'heartburn' is rather misleading. It has nothing to do with the heart. Or it has everything to do with the heart, only not the way you might think.

CHAPTER 58

Sometimes, people who, I think, mean well like to tell me I am not fat. They will say things like, 'Don't say that about yourself,' because they understand 'fat' as something shameful, something insulting, while I understand 'fat' as a reality of my body. When I use the word, I am not insulting myself. I am describing myself. These pretenders will lie, shamelessly, and say, 'You're not fat,' or offer a lazy compliment like, 'You have such a pretty face,' or 'You're such a nice person,' as if I cannot be fat and also possess what they see as valuable qualities.

It's hard for thin people to know how to talk to fat people about their bodies, whether their opinions are solicited or not. I get that, but it's insulting to pretend I am not fat or to deny my body and its reality. It's insulting to think I am somehow unaware of my physical appearance. And it's insulting to assume that I am ashamed of myself for being fat, no matter how close to the truth that might be.

CHAPTER 59

There are very few spaces where bodies like mine fit.

Chairs with arms are generally unbearable. So many chairs have arms. The bruises tend to linger. They remain tender to the touch hours and days after. My thighs have been bruised, more often than not, for the past twenty-four years. I cram my body into seats that are not meant to accommodate me, and an hour or two or more later, when I stand up and the blood rushes, the pain is intense. Sometimes, I'll roll over in bed and wince and then remember, yes, I sat in a chair with arms. Other times, I catch a brief glance of myself in the mirror, maybe while wrapping a towel around my body, and I see the pattern of bruising inching from my waist down to my midthigh. I see how physical spaces punish me for my unruly body.

The pain can be unbearable. Sometimes, I think the pain will break me. Anytime I enter a room where I might be expected to sit, I am overcome by anxiety. What kind of chairs will I find? Will they have arms? Will they be sturdy? How long will I have to sit in them? If I do manage to wedge myself between a chair's narrow arms, will I be able to pull myself out? If the chair is too low, will I be able to stand up on my own? This recitation of questions is constant, as are the recriminations I offer myself for putting myself in the position of having to deal with such anxieties by virtue of my fat body.

This is an unspoken humiliation, a lot of the time. People have eyes. They can plainly see that a given chair might be too small, but they say nothing as they watch me try to squeeze myself into a seat that has no interest in accommodating me. They say nothing when making plans to include me in these inhospitable places. I cannot tell if this is casual cruelty or willful ignorance.

As an undergraduate, I dreaded classrooms where I would have to wedge myself into one of those seats with the desk attached. I dreaded the humiliation of sitting, or half sitting, in such a chair, my fat spilling everywhere, one or both of my legs going numb, hardly able to breathe as the desk dug into my stomach.

At movie theaters, I pray the auditorium has been outfitted with movable armrests or I am in for some hurt. I love plays and musicals, but I rarely attend the theater because I simply cannot fit. When I do attend such events, I suffer and can barely concentrate because I am in so much pain. I beg off socializing a lot and friends think I am more antisocial than I really am because I don't want to have to explain why I cannot join them.

Before I go to a restaurant, I obsessively check the restaurant's website, and Google Images and Yelp, to see what kind of seating it has. Are the seats ultramodern and flimsy? Do they have arms, and if so, what kind? Are there booths, and if so, does the table move or is it one of those tables welded between two benches? How long do I think I can sit in those chairs without screaming? I do this obsessive research because people tend to assume that everyone moves through the world the way they do. They never think of how I take up space differently than they do.

Picture it. A dinner, two couples, a trendy restaurant. As we are seated, I quickly realize I haven't done my homework. The chairs are sturdy but narrow with rigid arms. I ask the hostess if we can sit at a booth, but even though the restaurant is empty, she says they are already all reserved. I want to cry but I can't. I'm on a date. We are with friends. My companion knows what I am feeling but also knows I wouldn't want any extra attention, knows I will endure the chair rather than make a scene. I am between a rock and a hard place.

We are seated and I perch myself on the edge of the seat. I have done this before. I will do it again. My thighs are very strong. I want to enjoy the meal, the lovely conversation with these treasured friends. I want to enjoy the cocktails and the gorgeous food being put before us, but all I can think about is the pain in my thighs and the arms of the chair pinching my sides and how much longer I will have to pretend everything is fine.

When the meal is finally over, relief washes over me. When I stand, I am dizzy and nauseated and aching.

Even the happiest moments of my life are overshadowed by my body and how it doesn't fit anywhere.

This is no way to live but this is how I live.

CHAPTER 60

I am always uncomfortable or in pain. I don't remember what it is like to feel good in my body, to feel anything resembling comfort. When walking through a door, I eye the dimensions and unconsciously turn sideways whether I need to or not. When I am walking, there is the twinge of my ankle, a pain in my right heel, a strain in my lower back. I'm often out of breath. I stop sometimes and pretend to look at the scenery, or a poster on the wall, or, most often, my phone. I avoid walking with other people as often as possible because walking and talking at the same time is a challenge. I avoid walking with other people anyway, because I move slowly and they don't. In public bathrooms, I maneuver into stalls. I try to hover over the toilet because I don't want it to break beneath me. No matter how small a bathroom stall is, I avoid the handicapped stall because people like to give me dirty looks when I use that stall merely because I am fat and need more space. I am miserable. I try, sometimes, to pretend I am not, but that, like most everything else in my life, is exhausting.

I do my best to pretend I am not in pain, that my back doesn't ache, that I'm not whatever it is I am feeling, because I am not allowed to have a human body. If I am fat, I must also have the body of someone who is not fat. I must defy space and time and gravity.

CHAPTER 61

And then there is how strangers treat my body. I am shoved in public spaces, as if my fat inures me from pain and/or as if I deserve pain, punishment for being fat. People step on my feet. They brush and bump against me. They run straight into me. I am highly visible, but I am regularly treated like I am invisible. My body receives no respect or consideration or care in public spaces. My body is treated like a public space.

CHAPTER 62

Air travel is another kind of hell. The standard economy-class seat is 17.2 inches while a first-class seat is, on average, between 21 and 22 inches wide. The last time I flew in a single coach seat, I was in an exit row, for the legroom. I fit in the seat because on that particular airline, Midwest Express, there was no window-seat armrest in the exit rows. I boarded and sat. Eventually my seatmate joined me, and I could instantly tell he was agitated. He kept staring at me and muttering. I could tell he was going to start trouble. I could tell he was going to humiliate me. I was mortified. He leaned into me and asked, 'Are you sure you can handle the seat's responsibilities?' He was elderly, rather frail. I was fat, but I was, I still am, tall and strong. It was absurd to imagine I could not handle the exit-row responsibilities. I simply said yes, but I wished I were a braver woman, the kind who would turn his question back on him.

When you are fat and traveling, the staring starts from the moment you enter the airport. At the gate, there are so many uncomfortable looks as people make it plain that they do not want to be sitting next to you, having any part of your obese body touching theirs. During the boarding process, when they realize that they have lucked out in this particular game of Russian roulette and will not be seated next to you, their relief is visible, palpable, shameless.

On this particular flight, the plane was about to pull away from the gate when this agitated man called for a flight attendant. He stood and followed her to the galley, from where his voice echoed through the plane as he said it was too risky for me to be seated in the exit row. He clearly thought my presence in the exit row meant the end of his life. It was like he knew something about the flight no one else did. I sat there and dug my fingernails into the palms of my hands as people began to turn and stare at me and mutter their own comments. I tried not to cry. Eventually, the agitated man was reseated elsewhere, and once the plane took off, I curled into the side of the plane and cried as invisibly, as silently, as I could.

From then on, I began to buy two coach seats, which, when I was still relatively young and broke, meant I could rarely travel.

The bigger you are, the smaller your world becomes.

The bigger you are, the smaller your world becomes.

Even when you've bought two coach seats, travel

is rife with humiliations. Airlines prefer that obese people buy two tickets, but few airline employees have any sense of how to deal with two boarding passes and the empty seat once a plane is fully boarded. It becomes a big production: first when you are boarding and they need to scan two boarding passes as if this is an unsolvable mystery and then, once you're seated, as they try to make sense of the discrepancy, no matter how many times you tell them, yes, both of these seats are mine. The person on the other side of the empty seat often tries to commandeer some of that space for themselves, though if any part of your body were touching them, they would raise hell. It's an unnerving hypocrisy. I get very salty about that, and the older I get, the more I tell people that they don't get to have it both ways – complaining if any part of my body dared to touch theirs if I bought one seat, but placing their belongings in the empty space of the empty seat I bought for my comfort and sanity.

And of course, there is the issue of the seat belt. I have long traveled with my own seat belt extender because it can be quite the ordeal to get one from a flight attendant. There are few discreet opportunities to request one. Flight attendants often forget if you ask when, say, boarding the plane. They tend to make a big show of handing it to you when they finally remember, as if punishing you, reminding everyone else on the plane that you are too fat to use the standard seat belt. Or that is what it feels like because I am so self-conscious about everything related to my body.

By carrying my own seat belt extender, I have often been able to circumvent these petty humiliations and nuisances, but there really is no escape. On recent regional flights, I have been told that it is airline regulation to use authorized extenders only. There was one particularly grim flight to Grand Forks, North Dakota, where the flight attendant made me remove my seat belt extender and take one from her, in front of the entire plane, before she would allow us to take off. Federal regulations, she said.

I am very lucky that I have finally gotten to a place in my career where it is part of my contract with an organization flying me to speak that they have to buy me a first-class ticket. This is my body and they know it, and if they want me to travel to them, they need to ensure at least some of my dignity.

This recitation feels so indulgent but this is my reality. This too is the truth of living in a fat body. It's a lot of weight to bear.

PART V

CHAPTER 63

In *Mastering the Art of French Cooking*, Julia Child writes, 'Cooking is not a particularly difficult art, and the more you cook and learn about cooking, the more sense it makes. But like any art it requires practice and experience. The most important ingredient you can bring to it is a love of cooking for its own sake.'

I did not think it was possible for me to love cooking. I did not think such a love was allowed. I did not think I could love food or indulge in the sensual pleasures of eating. It did not occur to me that to cook for myself was to care for myself or that I was allowed to care for myself amidst the ruin I had let myself become. These things were forbidden to me, the price I paid for being so wildly undisciplined about my body. Food was fuel, nothing more, nothing less, even if I overindulged in that fuel whenever I could.

But then I moved to Michigan's Upper Peninsula and lived in a town of about four thousand while attending graduate school. And after that I took my job in Charleston, Illinois, another small town. I became a vegetarian and realized that if I wanted to eat, I was going to have to prepare meals for myself or I would be relegated to a diet of iceberg lettuce and French fries.

Around that same time, I started watching *Barefoot Contessa*, Ina Garten's cooking show on the Food Network, every day from four to five p.m., just after I got home from campus. It was a time to let the world go and relax. I love the show. I love everything about Ina. Her hair is always glossy and smooth in a perfectly coiffed dark bob. She wears a variation on the same shirt every day. I learned from the FAQs on her website that her shirt is custom-made, but she won't divulge by whom. She is married to a man named Jeffrey who has a fondness for roast chicken, and if the show is any indication, their relationship is an adoring one. She is intelligent and wealthy and wears these traits comfortably but inoffensively.

Ina loves rhetorical questions. 'How good is that?' she'll ask while sampling one of her delicious dishes. Or, 'Who wouldn't want that for their birthday?' while planning a surprise for one of her coterie of elegant Hamptons friends. Or, 'We need a nice cocktail for breakfast, don't we?' when preparing brunch for some of her many always attractive, wealthy, and often gay friends. There is one episode where she takes food (bagels and lox) on a trip to Brooklyn to eat more food (at a farmer's market or some such).

I love Ina Garten so much one of my wireless

networks at home is named Barefoot Contessa. It's like she's watching over me that way.

Ina Garten makes cooking seem easy, accessible. She loves good ingredients – good vanilla, good olive oil, good everything. She is always offering helpful tips – very cold butter makes pastry dough better, and a cook's best tools are clean hands. She uses an ice cream scoop for the dough when she's making muffins and reminds the audience of this trick with a conspiratorial grin. When she shops in town, she always asks the butcher or fishmonger or baker to put her purchases on her account. She doesn't sully herself with cash.

One day, she invites some construction workers who are rehabbing a windmill over for lunch and she decorates the table with construction accessories like a tarp and some paintbrushes and a bucket. As she prepares their meal, she makes sure to provide man-sized portions, to be followed by a brownie pie, a decadent affair I would eventually try to bake.

What I love most about Ina is that she teaches me about fostering a strong sense of self and self-confidence. She teaches me about being at ease in my body. From all appearances, she is entirely at ease with herself. She is ambitious and knows she is excellent at what she does and never apologizes for it. She teaches me that a woman can be plump and pleasant and absolutely in love with food.

She gives me permission to love food. She gives

me permission to acknowledge my hungers and to try and satisfy them in healthy ways. She gives me permission to buy the 'good' ingredients she is so fond of recommending so that I might make good food for myself and the people for whom I enjoy cooking. She gives me permission to embrace my ambition and believe in myself. In the case of *Barefoot Contessa*, a cooking show is far more than just a cooking show.

CHAPTER 64

I am not the kind of person who can survey the pantry, identify four or five random ingredients, and assemble a delicious meal. I need the protection and comfort of recipes. I require gentle instruction and guidance. On a good day, I can experiment with a recipe, try to mix things up, but I need a foundation of some kind.

There is, I must admit, something very satisfying about making things from scratch, to know every dish in a meal was made by your own hands. As a lazy person, I'm a fan of premade things, but it was a lot of fun and deeply relaxing to make, for example, my own dough and my own cherry filling for a beautiful cherry pie. I felt productive and capable.

What has fascinated me about cooking, and coming to it in the middle of my life, is how it's actually a really good endeavor for a control freak. There are rules, and to succeed, at least in the early going, those rules need to be followed. I am good at following rules when I choose to.

I take particular pleasure in baking, which is a challenge because baked goods are generally not conducive to healthy eating or weight loss. But I teach, and so sometimes, I bake and bring treats to work to share with my students or colleagues.

Part of the pleasure of baking is in its precision. Unlike cooking, which favors experimentation, baking requires weighing and measuring and exact times and temperatures. The pleasure of having rules to follow is multiplied.

Things often go wrong and cooking can be messy, but the act of creating something from disparate ingredients still remains satisfying. Cooking reminds me that I am capable of taking care of myself and worthy of taking care of and nourishing myself.

CHAPTER 65

Food, itself, is complicated for me. I enjoy it, too much. I like cooking but hate grocery shopping. I'm busy. I am an embarrassingly picky eater. I am always trying to lose weight. This combination has me always in search of programs or products that will make it possible for me to manage dealing with all these issues at once. I tried a service called Fresh 20, which does the meal planning but leaves you responsible for the grocery shopping. I've tried Weight Watchers. I've tried eating only Lean Cuisines. I've tried low-carb diets. I've tried high-protein diets. I've tried combinations of various things. I've tried SlimFast during the day and one real meal at night. I've tried to keep healthy snacks around – fake junk food that only depresses me as it tries to serve as a plausible substitute for the real thing – beet chips, kale chips, pea crisps, rice cakes. Then I've thrown all that fake junk food out because I don't want fake junk food, I want real junk food, and if I cannot have real junk food, I'd rather have no junk food at all. I've tried to eat fruits and nuts. I've tried fasting every other day. I've tried eating all my meals before eight p.m. I've tried eating five small meals a day. I've tried drinking enormous quantities of water each day to fill my stomach. I've tried to ignore my hunger.

In truth, these attempts have always been either fairly half-assed or short-lived.

In my quest to better nourish myself, I joined Blue Apron when I moved to Indiana in 2014. Blue Apron is a subscription service, where each week, they send you the ingredients, in the correct portions, for three meals. They deal with two of the most unpleasant cooking-related tasks: meal planning and grocery shopping. I was kind of skeptical about meal kits because members are given little control over the meals they receive. But if I was going to try and take better care of myself, I was going to put my best foot forward.

It's really cute how everything is labeled and packaged. There are knickknacks that include things like tiny bottles of champagne vinegar and a little ramekin of mayonnaise. As someone who loves tiny things, I always considered unpacking the box something of an event. The ingredients are accompanied by full-color, full-page recipe cards with step-by-step instructions and pictures. There is little room for error, and yet there is still the human factor. I am the one who is left to prepare the meals, and my fallibility is particularly pronounced in the kitchen.

My first meal was a cannellini bean and escarole salad with crispy potatoes. I wasn't at all sure what escarole is, but I decided it was spicy lettuce, a better, more accurate name. The amount of spicy lettuce Blue Apron sent was laughable, so I added a head of romaine hearts because lettuce has no calories or nutritional value but it can take up some space on a plate.

The recipe was simple enough. I washed and peeled two potatoes, sliced them, boiled them for the prescribed amount of time. While that was happening, I made the dressing – mayonnaise, fresh squeezed lemon, garlic. The recipe also called for capers but I hate them, so slimy and ugly, and while I was trying to work through my pickiness, there was only so much progress to be made in one sitting.

When the potatoes were ready, they went onto a baking sheet and I drizzled them with olive oil, salt, and pepper. They baked at 500 degrees for twenty-five minutes and my kitchen got unbearably hot. I began thinking about the melancholy of cooking for yourself when you are single and living alone. One of the many reasons it took me so long to learn how to cook and learn to enjoy cooking is that it often feels like such a waste to go to all that trouble for myself.

Dinner would not wait for melancholy, so after rinsing and draining the beans, I softened a yellow onion, then assembled the salad, adding tomato, the beans, the lettuce, the dressing, all served over the crispy potatoes. It all turned out fine even though I had the saddest collection of kitchen tools aiding me in the process. It was the first time in my life something I prepared bore any resemblance to the recipe from whence it came.

In another box, there were ingredients for an English pea ravioli dish. I began by softening four cloves of garlic and some onion. The onion looked hideous because I do not have knife skills. What should have been orderly diced onion was a quantity of awkwardly shaped onion chunks. When the onion and garlic were softened, I added the English peas, some salt and pepper. It all smelled good. I felt accomplished, and maybe even a little powerful, the mistress of my culinary domain.

I took the onions and peas off the heat and added some chopped mint, and then added it to fresh ricotta, an egg, and some Parmesan cheese. This was, in theory, the filling for my ravioli.

It's interesting, I've noticed while cooking, how ingredients in their individual and naked state can be a bit repulsive but necessary, kind of like people. The egg, Parmesan, and ricotta, so wet and loose, did not thrill me. It felt way too intimate.

And then it came time to assemble the ravioli. I thought I followed the instructions correctly, but the ravioli did not reflect that. The assembly process itself was irritating. The pasta sheets wouldn't hold together, no matter what I tried. I crimped the edges with a fork, but the edges would not stay crimped. I nearly threw the disastrous-looking ravioli against a wall because the tenor of my aggravation was wildly dispropor- tionate to the potential of the meal I was attempting. In the end, I decided, *Fuck it*, and threw the sloppy mess into boiling water, hoping for the best, prepared to eat the worst.

The pockets of pasta I had tried to create quickly dissembled, coming apart limply at the seams. Tragedy was multiplying. Once I thought the pasta sufficiently cooked, I drained the whole mess into a strainer, and then put that mess in a saucepan with browned butter and let it simmer until it looked at least somewhat edible. The dissembled ravioli ended up tasting fine and I am sure there was a lesson in there somewhere about how almost anything can be salvaged when you cook, but I never did find that lesson.

Blue Apron and other meal kit services are well and good, but sometimes cooking is such a pain in the ass. It is exhausting wrapping my mind around having to prepare food to put in my body every single day, and living alone, I am always the one responsible for that preparation. The more I cook for myself, the richer my appreciation for women and men who cook for their families every day grows.

Some nights, it is a question of whether I have peanut butter, jelly, and bread so that the dinner problem is thusly solved. Of course, I cannot help but wonder when basic meals became problems rather than meals, complicated ordeals rather than daily, sustaining rituals. I love food, but it is so difficult to enjoy food. It is so difficult to believe I am allowed to enjoy food. Mostly, food is a constant reminder of my body, my lack of will-power, my biggest flaws.

CHAPTER 66

When I ask my mother for her recipes, she is, at once, helpful and vague. She shares the basic ingredients and cooking instructions, but I can never quite replicate the taste of her dishes. Once I asked her for a recipe for *soup joumou*, which Haitians prepare for New Year's Day, our Independence Day. This is what my mother offered.

Two heads of cabbage *Turnips*
Peas *Carrots*
Butternut Squash *Onions*
Leeks *Cilantro and Parsley*
Potatoes *Beef Tenderloin*

Cook meat until tender over low heat. Season to taste with garlic, salt, black pepper and hot peppers.

Add water.

Add vegetables.

I have never attempted this recipe.

My mother always insists she is giving me or my sisters-in-law the complete recipe, but I cannot shake the sense she is holding back, keeping a secret or two to herself so what is unique about her cooking, her affection for her family, will always be in her sole possession.

Sauce is the staple of many Haitian meals – tomato-based, fragrant, delicious. Even when my mother makes American food, sauce is on the table. It goes with everything. If my dad sits at the dinner table and doesn't see the sauce, he asks, 'Where is the sauce?' and my mother scowls. Sometimes, she is simply teasing him and the sauce is in the oven warmer. Sometimes, she isn't in the mood to make it.

I never seem to hold on to the most important elements of my mother's recipes, so when I am in my own home trying to cook certain Haitian dishes, I call home and she patiently walks me through the recipe. The sauce, a simple but elusive dish, stymies me. My mother reminds me to put on my cooking gloves. I pretend that such a thing would ever find a place in my kitchen. She tells me to slice onions and red peppers, setting the vegetables aside after a stern reminder to *wash everything*. My kitchen fills with the warmth of home. The sauce always turns out well enough but not great. I cannot place what, precisely, is off, and my suspicion that my mother has withheld some vital piece of information grows. As I eat the foods of my childhood prepared by my own hand, I am filled with longing and a quiet anger that has risen from my family's hard love and good intentions.

There is one Haitian dish I have mastered – our macaroni and cheese, which is filling but not as heavy as the American version. When I attend a potluck, an activity I dread because I am extraordinarily picky and suspicious of communal foods, I bring this dish. People are always impressed. They feel more cosmopolitan, I think. They expect there to be a rich narrative behind the dish because we have cultural expectations about 'ethnic food.' I don't know how to explain that for me the dish is simply food that I love, but one I cannot connect to in the way they assume. Instead of being a statement on my family's culture, this dish, and most other Haitian foods, are tied up in my love for my family and a quiet, unshakable anger.

And still, when I am with my family, when we become that island unto ourselves, I allow myself to be a part of them. I am trying to forgive and make up for lost time, to close the distances I put between us even though it was necessary, for a time, for me to be apart from them. These are the people who know not all of me but know enough, know what matters most. They continue to love me so hard and I love them hard in return.

Every New Year's Eve, we all convene in Florida and attend a gala at my parents' country club. There is a five-course meal – lots of tiny, twee dishes. There is drinking and dancing. Even surrounded by a hundred other people, we are unto ourselves. We return to my parents' house by one in the morning and the party continues – furniture moved, *konpa* music playing, more dancing, my brothers and cousin and me staring at the breathtaking spectacle of this family, the beautiful beast we become when we are together.

My hunger is particularly acute when I visit my parents. For one, they are minimalists when it comes to keeping food in the house. They travel a lot, so it doesn't make sense to keep fresh produce around, knowing it will likely spoil before it is eaten. And though they eat and, I am sure, enjoy a good meal, my parents are not people who take exceptional pleasure in food. They rarely snack. Any food in the house generally requires some kind of preparation.

But there is also the paranoia I develop. I feel like everything I do is being watched, scrutinized, judged. I deprive myself, to give the appearance of conforming, of making some small effort to become thinner, better, less of a family problem. Because that's what they tell me – my weight is a family problem. So, in addition to my body, I carry that burden too, knowing that my loved ones consider me their problem until I finally lose 'the weight.'

I start to crave foods, any foods. I get uncontrollable urges to binge, to satisfy the growing ache, to fill the hollowness of feeling alone around the people who are supposed to love me the most, to soothe the pain of having the same painful conversations year after year after year after year.

I am so much more than hungry when I am home. I am starving. I am an animal. I am desperate to be fed.

CHAPTER 67

I come from a beautiful family. They are thin, stylish, attractive. Often, when I am around them, I do not feel like I belong. I do not feel like I deserve to be among them. When I look at family photos, which I assiduously avoid, I think, *One of these things is not like the other*, and it is a haunting, lonely feeling, thinking you don't belong with the very people who know you in the truest, deepest ways.

My father is tall, lean, and lanky, with a distinguished air about him. My mother is petite, beautiful, and elegant. When I was a child, her hair cascaded down her back and was so long she could sit on it. She loves to wear heels. My brothers are tall and athletic, handsome – one of them knows it and will happily tell you about all his charms. And then there is me, ever expanding.

I cannot enjoy food around my family, but to be fair, food is not something I can enjoy around most people. To be seen while I am eating feels like being on trial. When we do eat together, my family watches me. Or I feel like they are watching me because I am hyper-self-conscious, because they are *concerned*. Or, more accurately, my family used to intently watch me eating, monitor me, try to control and fix me. Now, though they have largely resigned themselves to this state of my body, I will forever feel like they are watching me and looking right through me. They still want to *help* even as they hurt me. I accept this, or I try.

And then when I am introduced to new people who know my family, there is always this look on their faces of what I will charitably call shock. 'You're Roxane? You're the one I've heard so many wonderful things about?' they ask. And then I have to break their hearts by saying, 'Yes. I am, indeed, part of this beautiful family.'

I know the look well. I've seen it many, many times at family gatherings and celebrations. It's hard to take. It crushes whatever shreds of confidence I muster. This isn't in my head. This isn't poor self-esteem. This is what comes from years of being the fat one in the beautiful family. For so long I've never talked about this. I suppose we should keep our shames to ourselves, but I'm sick of this shame. Silence hasn't worked out that well.

Or maybe this is someone else's shame and I'm just being forced to carry it.

CHAPTER 68

When I was nineteen years old, I came out to my parents over the telephone. I was in the Arizona desert, far from them, living with a couple I barely knew, working the kind of job that would scandalize anyone who knew me. I had cracked up, quite literally. I had dropped out of my Ivy League college and run away, cutting off all contact with everyone whom I knew and loved and who loved me. I was having an emotional breakdown, but I didn't have the necessary vocabulary to explain myself or to understand why I was making such choices.

The second to last woman I loved during my twenties, Fiona, finally made the grand gesture I always wanted her to make after I moved on or convinced myself I had moved on, because she would never give me what I needed – commitment, fidelity, affection. We were still friends, but I was seeing someone else, Adriana, who was beautiful and kind and crazy, though we too would ultimately be incompatible. Adriana lived across the country and was visiting me in the Midwest. We were having a good time. We did not yet know the worst things about each other. As these things seem to go, something about Adriana's temporary presence in our city made Fiona realize I was almost beyond her grasp.

My relationship with Fiona had been largely unspoken. We spent all our time together. Sometimes we were intimate. We knew each other's families. She was single and developed infatuations and sometimes relationships with other women, and still, I was there. We were there. It was enough until it wasn't. And there was Adriana. She wanted to give me more and I let her even though I didn't have enough to give her.

During Adriana's visit, Fiona kept calling me. There was an urgency in her voice I had always wanted to hear. She *needed* me and I was in a complicated place where being needed was very attractive. At one point during her visit, I dropped off Adriana at a bookstore and ran to Fiona's house because she said she simply *had* to see me. I don't even remember what we talked about, but I do remember that when I went to pick up Adriana, I felt guilty, couldn't look her in the eye.

I had gotten in the habit, you see, of dating women who wouldn't give me what I wanted, who couldn't possibly love me enough because I was a gaping wound of need. I couldn't admit this to myself, but there was a pattern of intense emotional masochism, of throwing myself into the most dramatic relationships possible, of needing to be a victim of some kind over, and over, and over.

That was something familiar, something I understood.

When they finally tracked me down and we spoke, all my parents wanted to know was why I'd disappeared because they are good parents who love their children fiercely. They would never let me go, not really. I was too young and too messed up to realize what I was putting them through. For that, I still carry regret. I didn't know what to tell them. I couldn't say, 'I am completely broken down and losing my mind because something terrible happened to me,' though that was the truth. I thought about their faith and their culture. I told them the one thing that I thought might finally sever the bond between us. It's not that I didn't want my parents in my life, but I did not know how to be broken and be the daughter they thought they knew. I blurted out, 'I'm gay.' This too shames me, not my queerness, but how little faith I put in them and how warped my understanding of queerness was.

Saying I was gay wasn't true, but it wasn't a lie. I was and am attracted to women. I find them rather intriguing. At the time, I didn't know I could be attracted to both women and men and be part of this world. And, in those early days, I enjoyed dating women and having sex with them, but also, I was terrified of men. The truth is always messy. I wanted to do everything in my power to remove the possibility of being with men from my life. I failed at that, but I told myself I could be gay and I wouldn't be hurt ever again. I needed to never be hurt again.

My parents were not thrilled to hear that their only daughter was gay. My mother made a comment about how she knew because I once told her I wanted to get married in denim. I failed to see the connection. I expected my parents to turn their backs on me, but they did nothing of the sort. They asked me to come home and I couldn't go to them, not yet. I couldn't let them know how broken I was. Still, we were talking again. A few months later, I would go home, and they would welcome me. For some time, things wouldn't be right between us, but they wouldn't be wrong. And much later, things would be right, and they would see me for who I am, and welcome the women I loved into their home, and love me for who I am. I would realize that had always been the case.

The first woman I slept with was big and beautiful. I still remember how she smelled. Her skin was so soft. She was kind when I was starving for kindness. It was just a one-night stand at a party. Several CDs played during our tryst. It was an experience. My tongue tingles when I think of her name. The next woman I slept with I called my girlfriend, even though we barely knew each other. We met on the Internet, and I packed up my stuff, and I flew to Minnesota from Arizona to be with her in the dead of winter. I had a suitcase, no winter clothing, and it was so cold the locks on her car froze. I did not know such a thing was possible. She lived in a dark, cramped basement apartment where I couldn't stand all the way up because I was too tall. We were ridiculous and young. We lasted two weeks.

For the next several years I dated a string of women who were terrible in new and different ways. There was the woman who grabbed my arm so hard she left a bruise. There was the woman who enjoyed the outdoors, camping, and womyn's music festivals, all of which I found horrifying. There was the woman who cheated on me and left the evidence of the transgression in my car. The bathroom at an Olive Garden was involved, which only added insult to injury. There was the woman who told me she could see being with me in the future but didn't know how to be with me every day between now and that hypothetical future.

I was also terrible in new and different ways. I was equally if not more culpable in these relationships. I was far too insecure and needy, constantly needing affirmation that I was loved, that I was good enough to be loved. I was emotionally manipulative in trying to get that affirmation. I had terrible judgment with women because I labored under the delusion that a woman couldn't hurt me, not like a man could. If a woman demonstrated any interest in me, I reciprocated her feelings, a gut reflex. I fell into the dangerous trap of being in love with the idea of being in love. I wanted to be wanted and needed. Time and again,

I ended up with women who wouldn't or couldn't give me a fraction of what I desired. I ended up with women to whom I couldn't or wouldn't give a fraction of what they desired.

I performed my queerness so I could believe this half-truth I had told everyone, that I had told myself. I marched. I was here and queer. In the way of young queers of my day, I wore an excessive number of pride rings and pins and such. I slathered my car in stickers. I was passionately militant about any number of issues without fully understanding why.

To make matters worse, I was still attracted to men, often intensely. In bed with my girlfriends, I sometimes pretended I was with someone else, someone with a body harder in certain places, leaner in others. I told myself it was enough. I told myself everyone has fantasies. I hated myself for wanting men when men had hurt me so badly. I told myself I was gay. I told myself this was all I could have so I couldn't get hurt. I told myself I was stone. For quite some time, I touched but wouldn't allow myself to be touched. I was stone *and* untouchable. I seethed. I was swollen with desire, with a desperate need to be touched, to feel a woman's skin against my skin, to find release through pleasure. I withheld even that from myself. I punished myself. I was stone. I could not bleed.

Years later, I realized that I could bleed and I could make others bleed. At the end of Adriana's visit, I returned home after taking her to the airport, leaving her with the promise we would see each other again soon. It was a promise I kept before I broke another promise and then broke her heart. Fiona had written me beautiful letters telling me everything I always wanted to hear from her. I sat on my couch, reading her words over and over, shaking because, finally, I had everything I wanted from her in the palm of my hand, and because, even then, I knew I was going to push her away. All I needed to do was pick up the phone and dial a number. All I needed to do was say, 'Yes.'

CHAPTER 69

For far too long, I did not know desire. I simply gave myself, gave my body, to whoever offered me even the faintest of interest. This was all I deserved, I told myself. My body was nothing. My body was a thing to be used. My body was repulsive and therefore deserved to be treated as such.

I did not deserve to be desired. I did not deserve to be loved.

In relationships, I never allowed myself to make the first move because I knew I was repulsive. I did not allow myself to initiate sex. I did not dare want something so fine as affection or sexual pleasure. I knew I had to wait until it was offered, each and every time. I had to be grateful for what was offered.

I entered relationships with people who mostly tolerated me and occasionally offered me a trifle of affection. There was the woman who cheated on me and the woman who stabbed my favorite teddy bear with a steak knife and the woman who always seemed to need money and the woman who was too ashamed of me to take me to work parties.

There were men too, but they were mostly unmemorable and, frankly, I expected them to hurt me.

My body was nothing, so I let anything happen to my body. I had no idea what I enjoyed sexually because I was never asked and I knew my wants did not matter. I was supposed to be grateful; I had no right to seek satisfaction.

Lovers were often rough with me as if that was the only way they could understand touching a body as fat as mine. I accepted this because I did not deserve kindness or a gentle touch.

I was called terrible names and I accepted this because I understood I was a terrible, repulsive thing. Sweet words were not for girls like me.

I was treated so badly or indifferently for so long that I forgot what being treated well felt like. I stopped believing that such a thing existed.

My heart received even less consideration than my body, so I tried to lock it away but never quite succeeded.

At least I am in a relationship, I always told myself. *At least I am not so repulsive, so abject, that no one will spend time with me. At least I am not alone.*

CHAPTER 70

I am not good at romantic interactions that aren't furtive and kind of sleazy. I don't know how to ask someone on a date. I don't know how to gauge the potential interest of other human beings. I don't know how to trust people who do express interest in me. I am not the girl who 'gets the date' in these circumstances, or that's what I cannot help but tell myself. I am always paralyzed by self-doubt and mistrust.

Normally, I force myself to feel attraction to someone who expresses interest in me. It's mortifying to admit that, but it's also the truth. I doubt I am alone in this. I often think, *Maybe this is my last chance, my only chance. I better make it work.*

Having standards, or trying to have standards and sticking to them, has proven to be more difficult than I imagined. It is hard to say, 'I deserve something good. I deserve someone I actually like,' and believe it because I am so used to believing, 'I deserve whatever mediocrity comes my way.' In our culture, we talk a lot about change and growing up, but man, we don't talk nearly enough about how difficult it is. It is difficult. For me, it is difficult to believe I matter and I deserve nice things and I deserve to be around nice people.

I am also plagued by this idea that because I'm not a slender supermodel, I really have no business having standards. Who am I to judge someone whose opening salvo is 'hi u doing?' That is a literal message I have received on a dating site. This self-esteem issue has shaped so much of my romantic life. My past is littered with mediocrity. (I have had a couple great relationships too!) Most of the time, though, I end up in these long, deeply unsatisfying relationships.

Even when I am in a good relationship it is hard to stand up for myself. It is hard to express dissatisfaction or have the arguments I want to have because I feel like I'm already on thin ice by virtue of being fat. It is hard to ask for what I want and need and deserve and so I don't. I act like everything is always fine, and it's not fair to me or anyone else.

I am really trying to change this pattern and take a hard look at the choices I make and why. I don't want to be relieved when a relationship ends. I have things to offer. I am nice and funny and I bake really well. I no longer want to believe I deserve nothing better than mediocrity or downright shoddy treatment. I am trying to believe this with every fiber of my being.

I often tell my students that fiction is about desire in one way or another. The older I get, the more I understand that life is generally the pursuit of desires. We want and want and oh how we want. We hunger.

CHAPTER 71

Sometimes, I get so angry when I think about how my sexuality has been shaped. I get angry that I can draw a direct line between the first boy I loved, the boy who made me into the girl in the woods, and the sexual experiences I have had since. I get angry because I no longer want to feel his hands on my desires. I worry that I always will.

My first relationship was my worst relationship. I was desperately young. My first relationship was with the boy who turned me into the girl in the woods. He was a good boy from a good family living in a good neighborhood, but he hurt me in the worst ways. People are rarely what they seem. The more I got to know him, the more I realized that he was always showing who he really was and the people in his life either saw through him or closed their eyes. After that boy and his friends raped me, I was broken. I did not stop letting him do things to me and that remains one of my greatest shames. I wish I knew why. Or I do know why. I was dead, so nothing mattered.

Since then I've had many other relationships and

none nearly that bad, but the damage was done. My course was set. And it's a shame that the measure is what is not so bad instead of what is thriving and good. I look at some of my worst relationships and think, *At least they didn't hit me.* I work from a place of gratitude for the bare minimum. Since then I've never been in a relationship where I've had to hide nonconsensual bruises. I've never feared for my life. I've never been in a situation where I couldn't walk away. Does this make me a lucky girl? Given the stories I've heard from other women, yes, it does make me a lucky girl.

This is not how we should measure luck.

I have had good relationships, but it's hard to trust that because what I consider good doesn't always feel very good at all.

Or I am thinking about testimony I've heard from other women over the years – women sharing their truths, daring to use their voices to say, 'This is what happened to me. This is how I have been wronged.' I've been thinking about how so much testimony is demanded of women, and still, there are those who doubt our stories.

There are those who think we are all lucky girls because we are still, they narrowly assume, alive.

I am weary of all our sad stories – not hearing them, but that we have these stories to tell, that there are so many.

CHAPTER 72

In one of my past relationships, again in my twenties, things between us were not good but also not that bad. It was the kind of relationship that reminds me that sometimes emotional abuse is even worse than physical abuse. I don't mind getting knocked around. I don't say that cavalierly. There are simply some things to which I am numb. This person, though, wanted to break me down, which became interesting because I did not realize I could still be broken down further. Who knew? They did, I guess. They smelled it on me.

There was nothing dramatic or violent between us. It was simply that I faced a barrage of constant criticism. Nothing I ever did was good enough. I was in my twenties and desperately insecure, so I thought this was what all relationships were like. I thought this was what I deserved because I was so worthless.

I couldn't spend time with this person's colleagues without a rigorous critique of everything wrong with me that I needed to try and improve. Most of the time, as you might imagine, we were not together in public because I was just not good enough. I never looked nice enough. I talked too loud. I breathed too loud. I slept too loud. I was too warm while I slept. I moved too much while I slept. I basically stopped sleeping. I just hugged as small a sliver of the edge of the bed as I could and I stayed awake so my sleeping wouldn't be such a nuisance. I was always tired.

I didn't wash dishes correctly. There is a right way and a wrong way to wash dishes. I know that now. *Don't get water on the floor. Drain the dish rack. Be careful how you organize the dishes in the dish rack.* One of my favorite things to do now is to wash dishes any old way. I spill water on the floor and I smile because these are my fucking floors and these are my dishes and no one cares if there is water on the floor.

I didn't eat food correctly. I ate too fast. I chewed too loudly. I chewed ice too often. I didn't put things away correctly. I didn't arrange my shoes by the front door the right way. I swung my arms while walking. I would be told these things and then have to try and remember all the things I shouldn't do so I wouldn't be so upsetting by just existing. We would be walking, and I would remember, *Okay, hold your arms at your side. Do not swing your arms.* I would spend all my time just reminding myself, *Don't swing your arms.* And then I might get distracted and forget and accidentally let my arm move an inch or two and I would hear this exasperated sigh, so I would

251

redouble my efforts to make myself less upsetting to this person I loved. *DON'T SWING YOUR ARMS, ROXANE.* Sometimes, I catch myself trying not to swing my arms even now and I get so angry. I get so fucking angry and I want to swing my arms like a windmill. These are my arms. This is how I walk.

One day I went to a department store and got my makeup done. I thought I looked pretty. I wanted to look pretty for this person. I bought a bunch of makeup so I could be a better girl. I went to their house to surprise them and they looked me up and down and told me what else I could do to be more tolerable, more presentable to them. I stood there on the front porch, wanting my body to collapse in on itself. I had been so excited, so happy I had made myself pretty, and it wasn't good enough. I certainly didn't try that again. I went home with all my expensive makeup and my pretty face and then I cried that makeup off. The makeup is still in a yellow bag in my closet. Sometimes, I take it out and look at it but I don't dare use it.

When I get my makeup done for television appearances while I am promoting a book or when I am asked to comment on pop culture or the political climate, I feel like I'm wearing a mask I have no right to wear. The makeup feels far thicker than it really is. I feel like people are staring at me, laughing at me for daring to think I could do anything to make myself more presentable. And I remember how I felt the one time I tried to look pretty for someone, how it wasn't enough. The first chance I get, I scrub the makeup off. I choose to live in my own skin.

I was never going to be good enough, but I tried so hard. I tried to make myself better. I tried to make myself acceptable to someone who would never find me acceptable but kept me around for reasons I cannot begin to make sense of. I stayed because they confirmed every terrible thing I already knew about myself. I stayed because I thought no one else would possibly tolerate someone as worthless as me. I stayed through infidelity and disrespect. I stayed until they no longer wanted me around. I would like to think at some point I would have left, but we always want to think the best of ourselves, don't we?

But I am a lucky girl. I think most of my sad stories are behind me. There are things I will no longer tolerate. Being alone sucks, but I would rather be alone than be with someone who makes me feel that terrible. I am realizing I am not worthless. Knowing that feels good. My sad stories will always be there. I am going to keep telling them even though I hate having the stories to tell. These sad stories will always weigh on me, though that burden lessens the more I realize who I am and what I am worth.

CHAPTER 73

The thing is, though, loneliness, like losing control of my body, is a matter of accretion. Twelve years of living in very rural places, a lifetime of shyness and social ineptitude and isolation, these things make the loneliness build and build and it cloaks me, sometimes. It is a constant, unwelcome companion.

For so long, I closed myself off from everything and everyone. Terrible things happened and I had to shut down to survive. I was cold, I've been told. I often write stories about women who are perceived as cold and resent that perception. I write these women because I know what it's like to have so much warmth roiling beneath the skin's surface, ready to be found.

I am not cold. I wasn't ever cold. My warmth was hidden far away from anything that could bring hurt because I knew I didn't have the inner scaffolding to endure any more hurt in those protected places.

My warmth was hidden until I found the right people with whom to share it, people I could trust – friends from graduate school, friends I met through the writing community when I was first starting out, the people who have always been willing to see and take me exactly as I am.

I am not promiscuous with my warmth, but when I share it, my warmth can be as hot as the sun.

CHAPTER 74

Part of the reason relationships and friendships can be so difficult for me is because
there is a part of me that thinks I have to
get things just right. I have to say the right things
and do the right things or I won't be liked or
loved anymore. It's stressful, so then I engage
in an elaborate attempt at being the best friend
or girlfriend and get further and further away
from who I really am, someone with a good
heart, but also someone who may not always get
things right. I find myself apologizing for things
I shouldn't be apologizing for, things I am not
at all sorry for. I find myself apologizing for who
I am.

And even when I am with good, kind, loving
people, I don't trust that goodness, kindness, or
love. I worry that sooner or later, they will make
my losing weight a condition of their continued
affection. That fear makes me try harder to get
things right, as if I am hedging my bets.

All of this makes me very hard on myself, very
driven. I just keep working and working and
working and trying to be right, and I lose sight of

who I am or what I want, which leaves me in a less than ideal place. It leaves me . . . nowhere.

With age comes self-awareness, or something that looks like self-awareness, and so I try to be on the lookout for patterns of behavior, choices I'm making where I'm trying too hard, giving too much, reaching too intently for being right where right is what someone else wants me to be. It's scary, though, trying to be yourself and hoping yourself is enough. It's scary believing that you, as you are, could ever be enough.

There is an anxiety in being yourself, though. There is the haunting question of 'What if?' always lingering. What if who I am will never be enough? What if I will never be right enough for someone?

CHAPTER 75

My fat body empowers people to erase my gender. I am a woman, but they do not see me as a woman. I am often mistaken for a man. I am called 'Sir,' because people look at the bulk of me and ignore my face, my styled hair, my very ample breasts and other curves. It bothers me to have my gender erased, to be unseen in plain sight. I am a woman. I am large, but I am a woman. I deserve to be seen as such.

We have such narrow ideas about femininity. When you are very tall and wide and, well, I guess the tattoos don't help, you all too often present as 'not woman.' Race plays a part in this too. Black women are rarely allowed their femininity.

There is also a truth that runs deeper. For a very long time, I only wore men's clothes. I very much wanted to butch myself up because I understood that to look or present myself like a woman was to invite trouble and danger and hurt. I inhabited a butch identity because it felt safe. It afforded me a semblance of control over my body and how my body was perceived. It was easier to move through the world. It was easier to be invisible.

In relationships with women, presenting as butch meant that I didn't have to be touched. I could pretend I didn't want to be touched and I could stay safe. I could have more of the control I constantly crave.

It was a safe haven until I realized that I was playing a role rather than inhabiting an identity that felt true to me. People were seeing me but they weren't seeing me.

I started to shed that identity, but people continued to see only what they wanted to see. Today, the people who misgender me aren't doing so because they perceive a queer aesthetic. They're doing so because they don't see me, my body, as something that should be treated or considered with care.

CHAPTER 76

The body is not a fortress, no matter what we may do to make it such. This may be one of life's greatest frustrations, or is it humiliations? I spend a lot of time thinking about bodies and boundaries and how people seem hell-bent on ignoring those boundaries at all costs. I am not a hugger. I never have been and I never will be. I hug my friends, and do so happily, but I am sparing with such affections. A hug means something to me; it is an act of profound intimacy, so I try not to get too promiscuous with it.

Also, I find it awkward, opening myself up, allowing people to touch, to breach my fortress.

When I tell strangers I am not a hugger, some take this as a challenge, like they can hug me into submission, like they can will my aversion to hugs away by the strength of their arms. Oftentimes, they will draw me into their body, saying something condescending like, 'See, it isn't that bad.' I think, *I never thought it was*, and I stand there, my arms limply at my sides, probably grimacing, but still, they don't get the message that I am not a willing participant in this embrace. The fortress hath been breached.

At readings, eager fans often ask for hugs and I offer my right hand saying, 'I don't do hugs, but I do handshakes,' and their faces fall in disappointment as if a hug with me is the necessary currency for their attention. Or they say, 'I know you don't like hugs, but I'm going to hug you anyway,' and I have to dodge their incoming bodies as politely as I can.

Why do we view the boundaries people create for themselves as challenges? Why do we see someone setting a limit and then try to push? Once, I was at a restaurant with a large group of people and the waitress kept touching me. It was really fucking annoying because I don't want to be touched like that unless we are in a sexual relationship. Every time she passed by, she would rub my shoulders or run her hand down my arm and I kept getting more and more irritated but I said nothing. I never do. Do my boundaries exist if I don't voice them? Can people not see my body, the mass of it, as one very big boundary? Do they not know how much effort went into this?

Because I am not a touchy-feely person, I always feel this light shock, this surprise, really, when my skin comes into contact with another person's skin. Sometimes that shock is pleasant, like *Oh, here is my body in the world*. Sometimes, it is not. I never know which it will be.

CHAPTER 77

More often than not, I feel hopeless. I give up. I cannot overcome myself, my body, these hundreds of pounds shrouding my body. It is easier, I think, to be miserable, to remain mired in self-loathing. I don't hate myself the way society expects me to until I have a bad day and then I do hate myself. I disgust myself. I cannot stand my weakness, my inertia, my inability to overcome my past, to overcome my body.

This hopelessness is paralyzing. Working out and eating well and trying to take good care of myself start to feel futile. I look at my body, and I live in my body, and I think, *I will never know anything but this. I will never know anything better than this.*

And then I think, *If I am really this miserable, if my life really is this hard, why do I still do nothing?*

All too often, I look at myself in the mirror and all I can do is ask myself, *Why?* and *What is it going to take for you to find the strength to change?*

CHAPTER 78

One of the many things I have always loved about writing (not to be confused with publishing) is that all you need is your imagination. It doesn't matter who you are, you can write. Your looks, especially, don't matter. As a naturally shy person, I loved the anonymity of writing before my career took off. I loved how my stories didn't care about my weight. When I started publishing that writing, I loved that, to my readers, what mattered were the words on the page. Through writing, I was, finally, able to gain respect for the content of my character.

That changed when I started gaining a national profile, going on book tours, doing speaking engagements and publicity and television appearances. I lost my anonymity. It's not that my looks mattered but my looks mattered.

It's one thing to write as if you have no skin. It's another thing entirely when photography is involved. I have to have my photo taken often, which makes me cringe. Every part of me becomes exposed to the camera. There is no hiding the truth of me. Often, there is video and then my truth, my fatness, is amplified. As my career has taken off, my visibility has exploded. There are pictures of me, everywhere. I have been on MSNBC and CNN and PBS. When a certain kind of people see me on television, they take the time to e-mail me or tweet at me to tell me that I'm fat or ugly or fat *and* ugly. They make memes of me with captions like 'Typical Feminist' or 'The Ugliest Woman in the World.' Sometimes Google Alerts takes me to a forum of MRA acolytes or conservative assholes having a field day insulting my looks with a picture of me from an event or magazine. I'm supposed to let it go. I'm supposed to shrug it off. I'm supposed to remember that the kind of people who would do such cruel things are beneath my regard. I am supposed to remember that what they really hate is themselves.

When I was doing publicity for *Bad Feminist*, I was interviewed for the *New York Times Magazine*. They needed a picture to accompany the interview and were not at all interested in my head shot or a random snapshot from my phone. I went to New York and had a photo shoot in a fancy photographer's studio, where the receptionist, a tall and lithe young woman clearly modeling on the side, offered me water or coffee while I waited.

In the magazine, they used a full-length picture of me, from head to toe. I am staring at the camera thinking, *This is my body. This is what I look like. Stop being surprised.* It's the kind of picture I always avoid, as if somehow, I can separate myself from my body if I am only photographed from the waist or neck up. As if I can hide the truth of me. As if I should hide the truth of me.

The photographer was charming, handsome. He and his wife were remodeling a home in Hudson Valley. I learned this because he apologized for not being able to attend my event that night. I don't even know how he knew about my event. He asked me if I wanted to freshen my makeup, but I was not wearing any, so I just smiled and said, 'This is my face.' Before we got started he asked me what music I wanted to listen to and I blurted out, 'Michael Jackson,' because that is all that came to mind. A few moments later, Michael Jackson began piping through speakers and I felt like I was in the middle of a movie.

Things only became more surreal. The photographer had two assistants who would hand him the camera or lens he wanted. He told me where to stand and how to pose like an action figure. He wanted me to loosen up, but I am not good at loosening up when a camera is pointed at me. Eventually I got the hang of it and cracked a smile or two. I started to feel cool, like I was having a moment. Then I remembered what would happen when these images were published. I knew I would be mocked, demeaned and degraded simply for existing. Just like that, the moment was gone.

In the early days, before there were a lot of pictures of me available online, I would show up to an event and organizers would often look right through me. At one event, a gathering of librarians, a man asked if he could help me and I said, 'Well, I am the keynote speaker.' His eyes widened and his face reddened and he stammered, 'Oh, okay, I'm the man you're looking for.' He was neither the first person nor will he be the last to have such a reaction. People don't expect the writer who will be speaking at their event to look like me. They don't know how to hide their shock when they realize that a reasonably successful writer is this overweight. These reactions hurt, for so many reasons. They illustrate how little people think of fat people, how they assume we are neither smart nor capable if we have such unruly bodies.

Before events I get incredibly stressed. I worry that I will humiliate myself in some way – perhaps there won't be chairs I can fit in, or perhaps I won't be able to stand for an hour, and on and on my mind goes.

And then, sometimes, my worst fears do come true. When I was on book tour for *Bad Feminist*, I did an event in New York City at the Housing Works Bookstore to celebrate Harper Perennial's fiftieth anniversary.

There was a stage, two or three feet off the ground, and no staircase leading to it. The moment I saw it, I knew there was going to be trouble. When it came time for the event to begin, the authors with whom I was participating easily climbed onto the stage. And then there were five excruciating minutes of me trying to get onto it

266

too while hundreds of people in the audience stared awkwardly. Someone tried to help. Eventually a kind writer onstage, Ben Greenman, pulled me up as I used all the muscles I had in my thighs. Sometimes, my body is a cage in the most glaring ways. I was filled with self-loathing of an intense degree for the next several days. Sometimes, I have a flashback to the humiliation of that evening and I shudder.

After hauling myself up onstage, I sat down on a tiny wooden chair and the tiny wooden chair cracked and I realized, *I am going to vomit* and *I am going to fall on my ass in front of all these people.* After the humiliation I had just endured, I realized I was going to have to stay silent on both counts. I threw up in my mouth, swallowed it, and then did a squat for the next two hours. I am not sure how I did not burst into tears. I wanted to disappear from that stage, from that moment. The thing about shame is that there are depths. I have no idea where the bottom of my shame resides.

By the time I got back to my hotel room, my thigh muscles were shredded, but I was also impressed with how strong those muscles are. My body is a cage, but this is my cage and there are moments where I take pride in it. Still, alone in that hotel room, I sobbed and sobbed. I felt so worthless and so embarrassed. Words cannot convey. I sobbed because I was angry at myself, at the event organizers and their lack of forethought. I sobbed because the world cannot accommodate a body like mine and because I hate being confronted by my limitations and because I felt so utterly alone and because I no longer need the layers of protection I built around myself but pulling those layers back is harder than I could have ever imagined.

CHAPTER 79

There is a price to be paid for visibility and there is even more of a price to be paid when you are hypervisible. I am opinionated, and as a cultural critic I share my opinions regularly. I am confident in my opinions and believe I have a right to share my point of view without apology. This confidence tends to upset people who disagree with me. Rarely are my actual ideas engaged. Instead, my weight is discussed. 'You are fat,' they say. Or, because, for example, I share that I love tiny baby elephants in my Twitter bio, they make an elephant joke where I, of course, am the elephant.

While on a publicity tour in Sweden, I mentioned on Twitter that the Swedes had their own version of *The Biggest Loser*. A random stranger suggested I was the American export for the show. The harassment is a constant, whether I am talking about something serious or trivial. I am never allowed to forget the realities of my body, how my body offends the sensibilities of others, how my body dares to take up too much space, and how I dare to be confident, how I dare to use my voice, how

I dare to believe in the value of my voice both in spite of *and* because of my body.

The more successful I get, the more I am reminded that in the minds of a great many people I will never be anything more than my body. No matter what I accomplish, I will be fat, first and foremost.

CHAPTER 80

During my twenties, I was broke. I remember the payday loans with the outrageous interest. There was so much ramen. Filling the gas tank with like five dollars at a time. Phone getting cut off. No health insurance for years and rare visits to the doctor. I had to get a CAT scan once, I can't even remember why, and it took me years to pay off. I didn't go to the dentist for years. This is not a sad story because I am lucky. This is just life, and frankly, I've had it easy in terms of material comfort. I am privileged. I always have been. I had a safety net because my parents would never have let me starve or be homeless, but I was on my own, as an adult should be, and I was often very, very broke. I was writing and no one was interested in that writing. I know, now, that I was putting in the work. I still am, of course, but back then I was just beginning to figure out how to use my voice in both fiction and nonfiction. I had a lot to learn and so I wrote and wrote and wrote and read and read and read and I hoped. I was going to school and then working and getting better and better jobs and then more school, and I was becoming a better writer and, very slowly, a better person. I became less broke, and then I was fine, not making that much but making enough money to always be able to handle my business. Twice in the past nine years I have moved and moving is expensive, but I could afford it. The last time I stood in my empty apartment before heading out, I sobbed. That is not something I am prone to doing. I allowed myself to feel everything. I allowed myself to acknowledge how far I have come. This isn't bragging. This is an atlas.

During my twenties, my personal life was the hottest mess. The hottest. It will never be that messy again because I've grown up and I finally give enough of a damn about myself to avoid burning myself in that kind of fire. I'm still a mess, but I'm a different kind of mess now. I can generally identify what the mess is and where it's coming from. I am learning to ask for help, slowly. I am learning a lot of things.

My eyes are wide open. They are prepared for whatever they might see.

I try to keep all this feeling in a safe place, a neatly contained place, because that is where it will always have to stay. And then there is the intensity of want. Raw urges. Engulfing. Crushing. Tenderness and fierceness, both. Possession. The container is a lie. The container has been shattered. Someone has found the way to my warm. They have taken my atlas into their hands. They trace the wildly arcing lines from beginning to end.

PART VI

CHAPTER 81

I go to the doctor as rarely as possible because when I go, whether for an ingrown toenail or a cold, doctors can only see and diagnose my body. I have gone to an emergency care facility for a sore throat and watched as the doctor wrote, in the diagnosis section, first, 'morbid obesity' and, second, 'strep throat.'

Doctors generally adhere to the Hippocratic oath, where they swear to abide by an ethical code, where they swear to act, always, in their patients' best interests. Unless the patient is overweight. I hate going to the doctor because they seem wholly unwilling to follow the Hippocratic oath when it comes to treating obese patients. The words 'first do no harm' do not apply to unruly bodies.

There is the humiliation of simply being in the doctor's office, which is, all too often, ill-equipped for the obese body, despite all the public hysteria about obesity and health. Many scales cannot weigh patients who weigh over 350 pounds. Blood pressure cuffs are always too small, as are the threadbare hospital gowns. It is difficult to climb onto the exam table. It is difficult to lie back, to make myself vulnerable, to be splayed wide open.

There is the humiliation of the scale, of confronting that number or confronting a scale that cannot accommodate my size. And of course, there is the performance of trying to get to my 'actual' weight by kicking off my shoes and wishing I could take off all my clothes, cut off my hair, have my vital organs and skeleton removed. Then, maybe, I would be willing to be weighed, measured, judged.

When a nurse asks me to step on the scale, I often decline, tell her that I know how much I weigh. I tell her I am happy to share that number with her. Because when I do get on the scale, few nurses can hide their disdain or their disgust as my weight appears on the digital readout. Or they look at me with pity, which is almost worse because my body is simply my body, not something that demands pity.

In the examination room, I hold my hands in tight fists. I am on guard, ready to fight, and really, I do have to fight, for my dignity, for the right to basic medical treatment.

Because doctors know the challenges the obese body can contend with, they are surprised to learn I am not diabetic. They are surprised to learn I am not on a hundred medications. Or they are not surprised to learn I have high blood pressure. They look at that number and offer stern admonitions about the importance of losing weight and getting my numbers back under control. This is when they are happiest, when they can try and use their expertise to force me to discipline my body.

As a result, I don't go to the doctor unless it is absolutely necessary even though I now have good health insurance and have always had every right to be treated fairly and kindly. I don't go to the doctor even though I've had an undiagnosed chronic stomach condition that is, at times, debilitating, for at least ten years. Doctors are supposed to first do no harm, but when it comes to fat bodies, most doctors seem fundamentally incapable of heeding their oath.

CHAPTER 82

O n October 10, 2014, one of my greatest fears was realized. I was in my apartment, commenting on stories from the graduate student for whom I was serving as thesis adviser. I had been having stomach pain all that week, but I often have stomach pain, so I paid it little mind. Eventually, I went to the bathroom and experienced a very intense wave of pain. *I need to lie down*, I thought. When I came to, I was on the floor and I was sweaty, but I felt better. Then I looked at my left foot, which was facing in an unnatural direction, the bone nearly poking through the skin. I realized, *This is not good.* I closed my eyes. I tried to breathe, to not panic, to not think of everything that would happen next. At the same time, there was a plumbing crisis, but I couldn't cope with that and my fucked-up foot, so I just moved the plumbing issue to the corner of my mind.

When you're fat, one of your biggest fears is falling while you're alone and needing to call EMTs. It's a fear I have nurtured over the years, and when I broke my ankle that fear finally came true.

Thankfully, that night, I had my phone in my pocket, so I pulled myself into the anteroom of the bathroom, hoping for a signal. My foot was starting to hurt, but nowhere near as badly as I thought it should hurt based on years of watching medical dramas like *Chicago Hope*, *ER*, and *Grey's Anatomy*.

This was Lafayette, Indiana, a small town, so 9-1-1 answered promptly. While on the phone with the kind operator I blurted out, 'I'm fat,' like it was some deep mark of shame, and he smoothly said, 'That's not a problem.'

Many EMTs showed up and 83 percent of them were hot. They were kind and full of empathy, and they winced each time they looked at my foot. Eventually they sort of splinted it and dragged me out on this contraption and lifted me onto a gurney and from there it was fine. They had trouble finding a vein, so I ended up with bruises in all the wrong places. While waiting for the EMTs, I texted my person that I had an accident. I wanted to play it down, but I was slowly realizing I had really injured myself.

At the hospital, I got X-rays and the technician said, 'Your ankle is very, very broken,' which is not to be confused, I guess, with just regular broken. My ankle was also dislocated. They couldn't operate that night so they had to realign my foot. That is exactly as horrifying as you think it is. They gave me fentanyl, that stuff Michael Jackson took to sleep, and told me I wouldn't remember a thing. They were right. When I regained consciousness I asked, 'Are you going to do it now?' I got a nice little pat on my leg for that. I was grateful for the pharmaceutical industry.

Two other strange things were going on. My heart was beating in an irregular rhythm, which I am pretty sure has been the case for years, and I had a really low hemoglobin count. They were not going to send me home, so I got a room I would end up staying in for ten days. My ass became so sore I was ready to remove it surgically. I barely got any sleep, especially in the early going, so my mental state was not great. Every so often nurses would take my 'vitals' and poke and do other inscrutable things to me. I hate being touched, so that was a particular treat. They did, mercifully, have appropriately large hospital gowns, but it was a very small comfort. There is so much indignity to being helpless.

At this particular hospital, they took vitals at eleven p.m. and three a.m. and seven a.m., so I'm not sure when sleep was supposed to happen. They also took vitals throughout the day. I learned a great deal about hospital routines during those ten days. I basically became an expert. In the next room over was a woman who said, 'Hey,' every twenty or so seconds. She liked to pull out her IVs and was a troublemaker. She was elderly and I felt bad for her because I don't think anyone visited her the entire time. I was not so lucky.

The night of the accident, I had texted my sister-in-law and brother, who lived in Chicago at the time, and said, 'DON'T TELL MOM AND DAD,' because I knew my parents would panic. They did, of course, tell Mom and Dad. My parents did, in fact, panic. My brother and his wife rented a car and drove down to see about me. The first day was a blur of pain and confusion. The orthopedic surgeon couldn't operate because of my low hemoglobin, so I got my first blood transfusion. I marveled at how suddenly someone else's blood was inside of me. I also enjoyed that the orthopedic surgeon was incredibly attractive, knew it, and had the swagger of a man who is very good at what he does and very well compensated for that work. That was Saturday.

Sunday, I got another blood transfusion, so I carried the blood of at least two other people. Then the surgeon decided to operate because the ankle was unstable. When they rolled me to the operating area, I told the anesthesiologist that she should knock me out extra because I had seen the movie *Awake*. She shook her head and said, 'I hate that damn movie.' I told her I sympathized because movies about writers are uniformly terrible. Nonetheless, I said, 'But still, make sure I am super asleep.'

While all this was going on, I was communicating with my person on the phone, via text message. She was freaking out in the calmest way possible. She wanted to be in the hospital with me, but circumstances made that impossible. She was there in every way that mattered and I am still grateful for it.

In the operating room, I don't remember anything other than the oxygen mask descending upon my face. I woke up in another room to see a lady staring at me and I didn't want her staring at me so I said, 'Stop looking at me.' Then I went blank again. I heard from my brother that the surgery went well but that my ankle was even more broken than the doctor originally thought. A tendon was torn, this and that and the other. I have hardware in my ankle now. I am a cyborg.

My niece, with whom I am very close, eyed me suspiciously after surgery. She was two years old and not a fan of the huge cast on my left leg. She gave me a very reluctant air-kiss and went about her business. She also didn't like hospital beds. She did, however, like the rolling chair in the corner of my room. When I got back to my room after surgery, my parents had magically appeared, along with my other sister-in-law and niece and my cousin and his partner. I mean, talk about it taking a village. I was reminded, once again, that I am loved.

Over the course of the ten days, I listened to other people snoring very loudly, making growly sounds. The temperature fluctuated wildly. I became constipated. I wanted to shower very badly but couldn't. Instead, I was bathed by nurses' aides who had things like dry shampoo and the body-sized equivalents of moist towelettes. I was given a lot of good drugs and I really enjoyed that part. I had to face the severity of my injury and that I would be out of commission for quite some time. I had to cancel a few events and disappoint people, but I was going to be housebound for six weeks. I arranged, with my university, to teach my courses online while I recuperated.

I was well taken care of by the medical staff, but they were not good communicators. I became a throbbing mass of fear, loneliness, and neediness even though I was rarely alone for any amount of time. Everything was out of my control and I love control, so all my trigger points were being pressed at the exact same time.

I was absolutely terrified going into surgery. I realized I have so much life yet to live. I did not want to die. I thought, *I don't want to die*, and it was such a strange thought because I've never actively wanted to live as much as I did when I had to face my mortality in such a specific way. I began to think of all the things I still wanted to do, the words I had yet to write. I thought about my friends, my family, my person.

I don't do fear very well. I try to push the people I love away. I worry that I'm not allowed human weakness, that this makes me not good enough.

I was not at my best during the hospital stay because so much was out of my control and the bed was too fucking short and the hospital gown did not make me feel safe and I couldn't bathe and I couldn't really move and I wasn't eating because the hospital food was gross. I am not much of a crier, so I didn't really break down for several days, until one morning when the doctor told me I wasn't going home anytime soon.

I tried not to sob. I tried to cry in that neat way that delicate ladies cry in movies but . . . I am not a delicate lady. When a nurse would peer in, I'd rub my eyes and bite my lower lip so I might appear stoic, and then when they looked away, I'd start crying again. I babbled all kinds of sorrowful stuff. It was a low point, one of many.

Everyone was so worried about me when I broke my ankle and it confused me. I have a huge, loving family and a solid circle of friends, but these things were something of an abstraction, something to take for granted, and then all of a sudden, they weren't. There were people calling me every day and hovering over my hospital bed and sending me things just to cheer me up. There were lots of concerned texts and e-mails, and I had to face something I've long pretended wasn't true, for reasons I don't fully understand. If I died, I would leave people behind who would struggle with my loss. I finally recognized that I matter to the people in my life and that I have a responsibility to matter to myself and take care of myself so they don't have to lose me before my time, so I can have more time. When I broke my ankle, love was no longer an abstraction. It became this real, frustrating, messy, necessary thing, and I had a lot of it in my life. It was an overwhelming thing to realize. I am still trying to make sense of it all even though it has always been there.

It has now been more than two years. There is a throbbing in my left ankle that reminds me, 'Once, these bones were shattered.'

I always wonder what healing really looks like – in body, in spirit. I'm attracted to the idea that the mind, the soul, can heal as neatly as bones. That if they are properly set for a given period of time, they will regain their original strength. Healing is not that simple. It never is.

Years ago, I told myself that one day I would stop feeling this quiet but abiding rage about the things I have been through at the hands of others. I would wake up and there would be no more flashbacks. I wouldn't wake up and think about my histories of violence. I wouldn't smell the yeasty aroma of beer and for a second, for several minutes, for hours, forget where I was. And on and on and on. That day never came, or it hasn't come, and I am no longer waiting for it.

A different day has come, though. I flinch less and less when I am touched. I don't always see gentleness as the calm before the storm because, more often than not, I can trust that no storm is coming. I harbor less hatred toward myself. I try to forgive myself for my trespasses.

In my novel, *An Untamed State*, after Miri, my protagonist, has been through hell, she thinks about

287

how sometimes broken things need to be broken further before they can truly heal. She wants to find something that will break her in that necessary way so she can get back to the life she had before she was kidnapped.

I was broken, and then I broke my ankle and was forced to face a lot of things I had long ignored. I was forced to face my body and its frailty. I was forced to stop and take a breath and give a damn about myself.

I have always worried that I am not strong. Strong people don't find themselves in the vulnerable situations I have found myself in. Strong people don't make the mistakes I make. This is some nonsense I have cooked up over the years, notions I would disabuse anyone else of but somehow still carry myself. When I worry I'm not strong, I become very invested in appearing invulnerable, unbreakable, stone-cold, a fortress, self-sustaining. I worry that I need to keep up this appearance even when I cannot.

Before October 10, 2014, I was running myself into the ground. I have always run myself into the ground, been relentless, pushed and pushed, thought myself superhuman. You can do that when you're twenty, but when you're forty, the body basically says, 'Get a grip. Have a seat. Eat some vegetables and take your vitamins.' I came to many realizations in the aftermath of breaking my ankle. The most profound of those realizations was that part of healing is taking care of your body and learning how to have a humane relationship with your body.

I was broken and then I broke some more, and I am not yet healed but I have started believing I will be.

CHAPTER 83

I sort of knew, when I published my novel, that things would change, but I was pretty passive about it, partly because I was a little resentful that when a woman writes, her personal story becomes part of the story, even though the novel is fiction.

My parents have always known I was a writer. As a young girl they encouraged my creativity, got me my first typewriter, read the little stories I wrote, and praised them as loving parents do. But my writing was also something vague to them, particularly when I was an unknown writer without a book in, say, Barnes & Noble. They weren't familiar with the online magazines where most of my work was published, and I didn't go out of my way to share my work with them. When my story 'North Country' was included in *The Best American Short Stories*, I told my mother and she asked, 'What's that?'

I was pretty vague about the release of *An Untamed State* and *Bad Feminist*. I was particularly silent on the revelations to be found in *Bad Feminist*. And then *Time* magazine reviewed it and referenced my rape, which is not a secret to anyone who has read some of my essays but was, at the time, a secret to most of my family. What happened is not something I discussed with my family. I couldn't talk about it with them – it was too much. The memories are too fresh even now. The consequences are still with me. Or it was a secret.

The day he read the article online, my dad called and said, 'I read the *Time* review.' I was nonchalant, but I knew what he was getting at.

A few weeks earlier, my mom had poked at me, in her way, and we had a conversation about how sometimes children, even ones with great parents, are too scared to talk to their parents about the trauma they experience. I told her that most of my writing is about sexual violence and trauma. We talked about how we hoped the world would be better to my niece, and that if anything happened to her, she would talk to someone. I realized my mother knew and I was grateful that she and I are so similar and that it was enough to talk around the truth rather than stare it down.

When I went to visit my parents after the *Time* article, my dad asked, 'Why didn't you tell us about what happened?' and I said, 'Dad, I was scared.' I said, 'I thought I would get in trouble.'

When I was twelve, I was so ashamed of what had happened, of everything I had done with a boy I wanted to love me leading up to what happened with him and all his friends, of the aftermath. I felt like it was my fault.

My father told me I deserved justice. He told me he would have gotten justice for me, and I went inside myself as I all too often do. I went through the motions of the rest of the conversation, punctuated by a lot of staring at an electronic device. I could have handled it better, but I was hearing what I have needed to hear for so very long and I wanted to break down, though I don't know how to do that anymore. My family knows my secret. I am freed, or part of me is freed and part of me is still the girl in the woods. I may always be that girl. My dad and brothers want names. I will not speak his name.

My family understands me more now, I think, and that's good. I want them to understand me.

I want to be understood.

CHAPTER 84

Some years ago, I looked up this boy from my past, wanted to know what had become of him. He does not have an uncommon name, but his name isn't John Smith, either, so I had a chance. I looked and looked and looked. It became a minor obsession. Every day I scrolled through the hundreds of hits that came up when I searched his name on Google. I tried combinations of his name and the state where I knew him, but he no longer lives there. I tried to guess what he had become when he grew up – my first two guesses were politician or lawyer, so you can probably guess the kind of person he is. I found him. He is neither a politician nor a lawyer, but I wasn't far off. People don't change. I wondered if I would recognize him. I shouldn't have. There are some faces you don't forget. He looks exactly the same. Exactly. He looks older, but not by much. His hair is darker. I know how long it has been since I last saw him in years, months, and days. It has been more than twenty years but fewer than thirty. I would recognize him anywhere. He wears his hair in the same style he always has, real glossy-catalog preppy. He has a wide face. He's an executive at a major company. He has a fancy title. He has the same smug facial expression, that sort of 'the world is mine' cockiness innate to some people, people like him. Ever since I found him, I Google him every few days or so like I'm trying to make sure he doesn't go missing. I need to know where he is. I need to understand, at all times, the distance between him and me, just in case. I don't know why I'm telling you this. Or I do. I Googled him when I wrote this book. I don't know why. Or I do. I sat for hours, staring at his picture on his webpage on his company's website. It nauseates me. I can smell him. This is what the future brings. I think about tracking him down the next time I'm in his city. I am there sometimes. If I told my friends there what I was doing, they would try to stop me, so I would wait and keep my plans to myself, commit a sin of omission. I am good at waiting. I could make the time to find him. He wouldn't recognize me. I was skinny when he knew me and much shorter. I was very small and cute and smart but not smart. I am not that girl anymore. I could find him and hide in plain sight. I saw to that. He wouldn't see me. He would look right through me. I know where he works and his e-mail address and his phone number and fax number. I don't have these things written down, but I know. I have them bookmarked and maybe committed to memory. I know what the street outside his office building looks like because of

Google Maps Street View. There are lush trees. He has a nice view. This is the future. I don't have anything to say to him or, rather, anything I would say to him. Or I do. Maybe I have everything to say to him. I don't know. I wonder where he lives. If I went to his workplace and waited outside the parking lot and followed him home, I could find out where he lives, how he lives. I could see where and how he sleeps at night. I wonder if he's married, if he has children, if he's happy. Is he a good husband and father? I wonder if he keeps in touch with the guys he used to run with. I wonder if they ever talk about the good old days, if they talk about me. I wonder if he could tell me their names because I didn't really know them, I just knew of them, and then I did know them but never their names. I wonder if he has become a good person. This one time, we were making out in the woods and my younger brother caught us and then blackmailed me for weeks. I had to do what he said or he would tell on me, which meant doing all his stupid chores and worrying, constantly, that he would tell my parents I was a bad Catholic girl. Sibling relationships are strangely corrupt. My younger brother also told me, then, that he didn't like this guy and I should stay away. I told him he was being silly, immature. I had a secret romance with a golden boy. That's all that mattered. I told him he was jealous someone liked me. I told my brother he was just a kid, he couldn't under-stand. I should have listened to my brother. I was a kid too. I wonder how this man from my past takes his coffee because there is a Starbucks down the street from his office. Google showed me that too. I wonder if he eats red meat and if he still likes to look at *Playboy*s and if he has any hobbies and if he's still mean to fat kids. I was crazy for him. I probably would have done anything if he had bothered to ask. Do people still like him as much as they used to? What kind of car does he drive? Is he close to his parents? Do they live in the same house? I have called his office and asked for him. I have done this more than once. Mostly I hang up immediately. His secretary put me through once after I made up a story about why I needed to speak to him. It was a good story. When I heard his voice I dropped the phone. His voice hasn't changed. When I picked up the phone again, he kept saying, 'Hello, hello, hello . . .' This went on for a long time. He wouldn't stop saying hello. It was like he knew it was me, like he had been waiting too, and then after a long time he stopped saying hello and we sat there in silence and I kept waiting for him to hang up but he didn't and neither did I so we just listened to each other breathing. I was paralyzed. I wonder if he thinks of me, of what I gave him before he took what I did not. I wonder if he thinks of me when he makes love to his wife. Is he disgusted with himself? Does he get turned on when he thinks of what he did? Do I disgust him? I wonder if he knows I think of him every day. I say I don't, but

I do. He's always with me. Always. There is no peace. I wonder if he knows I have sought out men who would do to me what he did or that they often found me because they knew I was looking. I wonder if he knows how I found them and how I pushed away every good thing. Does he know that for years I could not stop what he started? I wonder what he would think if he knew that unless I thought of him I felt nothing at all while having sex, I went through the motions, I was very convincing, and that when I did think of him the pleasure was so intense it was breathtaking. I wonder if he is familiar with the Sword of Damocles. He is always with me, every night, no matter whom I'm with, always. If I were to track him down, I could pretend to be a client looking for what he deals in. I know how to move in his circles. I could make an appointment to have him show me things. I can afford to be in the same room as him even though I doubt he would have ever imagined that. I have a fancy title too. I could sit across from him in what must be a corner office with a view. I have no doubt his desk is huge and imposing and compensating for something. I wonder how long we would have to sit there before he recognized me. I wonder if he would even remember me. My eyes haven't changed. My lips haven't changed. If he remembered me, would he admit it, or would he pretend he didn't to try to feel me out, figure out my endgame? I wonder how long I would sit there. I wonder how long I could sit there. I wonder if I would tell him what I became, what I made of myself, what I made of myself despite him. I wonder if he would care, if it would matter.

CHAPTER 85

I am taking small steps toward the life I want. For the past twelve years, I have lived, rather unhappily, in rural America. As a black woman, this has been trying, at best. If I'm being honest with myself, other than graduate school, where I didn't have a choice in where I lived, I have been hiding. I'm afraid to live in a city where, at least in my mind, everyone is thin, athletic, beautiful, and I am an abominable woman.

I spent five years in Michigan's Upper Peninsula – a place I didn't even know existed until I moved there to attend graduate school. I lived in a town of four thousand people. The next town over, over the portage bridge, had seven thousand people. In my town, the street signs were in both English and Finnish because the town had the highest concentration of Finns outside of Finland. We were so far north that my blackness was more a curiosity than a threat. I was a woman out of place, but I did not always feel unsafe. There were the abandoned copper mines and the vast majesty of Lake Superior and so much forest cloaking everything. During fall, deer hunting, so much venison. The winters were endless, snow in unfathomable quantities, the aching whine of snowmobiles. There was loneliness. There were my friends, who made the isolation bearable. There was a man who made everything beautiful.

In rural Illinois, I lived in a town surrounded by cornfields, in an apartment complex next to an open meadow, the site of ambition thwarted when the developer who built the complex ran out of money. The meadow was wide and green, bordered by trees. In the fall, I often saw a family of deer galloping across the field. They reminded me of Michigan. Especially early on, they made me think, *I want to go home*, and I would startle, that my heart, my body, considered such an unexpected place home. The man didn't follow. The man didn't understand why I would not, could not, raise brown children in the only place he had ever called home. There was more to it, but there was also that. At the end of every summer, a farmer threshed the meadow and hauled the hay away. I stood on my balcony and watched as he worked, methodically, making the land useful. I had a job, I kept telling myself. At least I had a job. This town was bigger. I nurtured a very small dream – to live in a place where I could get my hair done – without knowing if that dream would ever come true. There was a Starbucks, though not much else. There was loneliness. There were a few very, very unsuitable men who made everything ugly. We were three hours from Chicago, so my blackness was less of a curiosity, more of a threat. And there were the black students on campus, the nerve of them, daring to pursue higher education. In the local newspaper, residents wrote angry letters about a new criminal element – the scourge of youthful black ambition, black joy. In my more generous moments, I tried to believe the locals were using anger to mask their fear of living in a dying town in a changing world.

Four years later, I moved to central Indiana, a much bigger town, a small city really. In the first weeks, I was racially profiled in an electronics store. Living here never got better. When I lamented how uncomfortable I was and am here, local acquaintances often tried to tell me, in different ways, 'Not all Hoosiers,' much in the same way men on social media would say, 'Not all men,' to derail discussions about misogyny. There is loneliness. The confederacy is alive and well here though we are hundreds of miles from the Old South. There is a man who drives around in an imposing black pickup truck with white-supremacist flags flying from the rear. My dental hygienist tells me I live in a bad part of town. There are no bad parts of town here, not really. In the local newspaper, residents write angry letters about a new criminal element in town. 'People from Chicago,' they say, which is code for black people. On campus, pro-life students chalk messages on sidewalks like 'Planned Parenthood #1 Killer of Black Lives' and 'Hands up, don't abort.' My blackness is, again, a threat. I don't feel safe, but I know how lucky I am, which leaves me wondering how unsafe black people leading more precarious lives must feel.

Friends in cities have long asked me how I do it – spending year after year in these small towns that are so inhospitable to blackness. I say I'm from the Midwest, which I am, and that I have never lived in a big city, which is also true. I say that the Midwest is home even if this home does not always embrace me, and that the Midwest is a vibrant, necessary place. I say I can be a writer anywhere, and as an academic, I go where the work takes me. Or, I said these things. Now, I am simply weary. I say, 'I hate it here,' and a rush of pleasure fills me. I worry that I can't be happy or feel safe anywhere. But then I travel to places where my blackness is unremarkable, where I don't feel like I have to constantly defend my right to breathe, to be. I am nurturing a new dream of a place I already think of as home – bright sky, big ocean. I'm learning to make a home for myself based on what I want and need, in my heart of hearts. I've decided that I will not allow my body to dictate my existence, at least, not entirely. I will not hide from the world.

CHAPTER 86

My body and the experience of moving through the world in this body has informed my feminism in unexpected ways. Living in my body has expanded my empathy for other people and the truths of their bodies. Certainly, it has shown me the importance of inclusivity and acceptance (not merely tolerance) for diverse body types. It has shown me that being a woman of size, the phrase I use to discreetly inform others of my body in a way that offers a semblance of dignity, is as much a part of my identity, and has been for at least twenty years, as any other part of my identity. Despite the frustrations and humiliations and challenges, I also try to find ways to honor my body. This body is resilient. It can endure all kinds of things. My body offers me the power of presence. My body is powerful.

And also, my body has forced me to be more mindful of how other bodies, of differing abilities, move through the world. I don't know if fat is a disability, but my size certainly compromises my ability to be in certain spaces. I cannot climb too many stairs, so I am always thinking about access to space. Is there an elevator? Are there stairs to the stage? How many? Is there a handrail? That I have to ask myself these questions shows me a fraction of the questions people with disabilities must ask to be out in the world. It shows me just how much I take for granted, how much we all take for granted when we are able-bodied.

During an event with Gloria Steinem, as she was promoting her book *My Life on the Road*, we were sitting onstage in Chicago. I was trying to maintain my cool because it was Gloria Steinem sitting next to me. A few feet to our right was the sign language interpreter. As Gloria and I began to talk, we noticed that there was some rumbling in the audience. Several people wanted the interpreter to move so they could better see Gloria and me. Their request was understandable in that sight lines are important. But those sight lines were certainly not more important than the interpreter being visible to the hearing-impaired. The interpreter stood and looked around the stage, clearly confused and distressed. I told her to sit right where she was, and that others being able to see us was not as important as her being seen. It was a conversation, after all. What mattered was that we could be heard by *everyone* in the audience.

I don't share this story because I am special or in need of congratulation. Instead this was one of those moments when I had a greater sensitivity that could only be brought about by the realities of my body. It was a moment when I understood that all of us have to be more considerate of the realities of the bodies of others.

I was and am thankful for that moment. I am thankful that my body, however unruly it is, allowed me to learn from that moment.

CHAPTER 87

I often wonder who I would have been if this terrible thing had not happened to me, if I hadn't spent so much of my life hungering so much. I wonder what Other Roxane's life would be like, and when I imagine this woman who somehow made it to adulthood unscarred, she is everything I am not. She is thin and attractive, popular, successful, married with a child or two. She has a good job and an amazing wardrobe. She runs and plays tennis. She is confident. She is sexy and desired. She walks down the street with her head held high. She isn't always scared and anxious. Her life isn't perfect, but she is at peace. She is at ease.

Or put another way, I've been thinking a lot about feeling comfortable in one's body and what a luxury that must be. Does anyone feel comfortable in their bodies? Glossy magazines lead me to believe that this is a rare experience, indeed. The way my friends talk about their bodies also leads me to that same conclusion. Every woman I know is on a perpetual diet. I know I don't feel comfortable in my body, but I want to and that's what I am working toward. I am working toward abandoning the damaging cultural messages that tell me my worth is strictly tied up in my body. I am trying to undo all the hateful things I tell myself. I am trying to find ways to hold my head high when I walk into a room, and to stare right back when people stare at me.

I know that it isn't merely weight loss that will help me feel comfortable in my body. Intellectually, I do not equate thinness with happiness. I could wake up thin tomorrow and I would still carry the same baggage I have been hauling around for almost thirty years. I would still bear the scar tissue of many of those years as a fat person in a cruel world.

One of my biggest fears is that I will never cut away all that scar tissue. One of my biggest hopes is that one day, I will have cut away most of that scar tissue.

CHAPTER 88

When I was twelve years old I was raped and then I ate and ate and ate to build my body into a fortress. I was a mess and then I grew up and away from that terrible day and became a different kind of mess – a woman doing the best she can to love well and be loved well, to live well and be human and good.

I am as healed as I am ever going to be. I have accepted that I will never be the girl I could have been if, if, if. I am still haunted. I still have flashbacks that are triggered by the most unexpected things. I don't like being touched by people with whom I do not share specific kinds of intimacy. I am suspicious of groups of men, particularly when I am alone. I have nightmares, though with far less frequency. I will never forgive the boys who raped me and I am a thousand percent comfortable with that because forgiving them will not free me from anything. I don't know if I am happy, but I can see and feel that happiness is well within my reach.

But.

I am not the same scared girl that I was. I

have let the right ones in. I have found my voice.

I am learning to care less what other people think. I am learning that the measure of my happiness is not weight loss but, rather, feeling more comfortable in my body. I am increasingly committed to challenging the toxic cultural norms that dictate far too much of how women live their lives and treat their bodies. I am using my voice, not just for myself but for people whose lives demand being seen and heard. I have worked hard and am enjoying a career I never dared think possible.

I appreciate that at least some of who I am rises out of the worst day of my life and I don't want to change who I am.

I no longer need the body fortress I built. I need to tear down some of the walls, and I need to tear down those walls for me and me alone, no matter what good may come of that demolition. I think of it as undestroying myself.

Writing this book is the most difficult thing I've ever done. To lay myself so vulnerable has not been an easy thing. To face myself and what living in my body has been like has not been an easy thing, but I wrote this book because it felt necessary. In writing this memoir of my body, in telling you these truths about my body, I am sharing my truth and mine alone. I understand if that truth is not something you want to hear. The truth makes me uncomfortable too. But I am also saying, here is my heart, what's left of it. Here I am showing you the ferocity of my hunger. Here I am, finally freeing myself to be vulnerable and terribly human. Here I am, reveling in that freedom. Here. See what I hunger for and what my truth has allowed me to create.